Poverty and Hunger

A World Bank Policy Study

Why is the food of the people so scarce? . . . Where does the blame lie? . . . I have been unable to attain a proper balance between important and unimportant affairs. Let this matter be debated. . . . Let all exhaust their efforts and ponder deeply whether there is some way to aid the people.

Edict of Emperor Wen
on the Primacy of Agriculture (163 B.C.)

It is no longer the simple field, however big, but the whole world which is required to nourish each one of us.

Teilhard de Chardin
The Phenomenon of Man

Poverty and Hunger

*Issues and Options
for Food Security
in Developing Countries*

The World Bank
Washington, D.C., U.S.A.

Copyright © 1986 by The International Bank
for Reconstruction and Development/The World Bank
1818 H Street, N.W., Washington, D.C. 20433, U.S.A.

All rights reserved
Manufactured in the United States of America
First printing February 1986

The map used in this document is solely for the convenience of the reader and does not imply the expression of any opinion whatsoever on the part of the World Bank or its affilates concerning the legal status of any country, territory, city, area, or of its authorities, or concerning the delimitation of its boundaries or national affiliation.

Library of Congress Cataloging-in-Publication Data

Poverty and hunger.

(A World Bank policy study)
Bibliography: p.
1. Food supply—Developing countries.
I. International Bank for Reconstruction and
Development. II. Series.
HD9018.D44P68 1986   363.8'09172'4   86-1583
ISBN 0-8213-0678-2

Poverty and Hunger

Issues and Options for Food Security
in Developing Countries

ERRATA

Page 23: in Table 2-8, the headings of the last two columns should be reversed so that they read *Production plus net imports* and *Net imports*.

Page 32: in the last line of the first column, substitute "output" for "price."

Foreword

Food security has to do with access by all people at all times to enough food for an active and healthy life. Available data suggest that more than 700 million people in the developing world lack the food necessary for such a life. No problem of underdevelopment may be more serious than, or have such important implications for, the long-term growth of low-income countries.

Attempting to ensure food security can be seen as an investment in human capital that will make for a more productive society. A properly fed, healthy, active, and alert population contributes more effectively to economic development than one which is physically and mentally weakened by inadequate diet and poor health.

Problems in food security do not necessarily result from inadequate food supplies, as is widely believed, but from a lack of purchasing power on the part of nations and of households. Economic growth will ultimately provide most households with enough income to acquire enough food. Supporting economic growth with an equitable distribution of income is therefore the first priority, and should continue as the main goal, of economic policy. But there are two well-known difficulties: economic growth takes time, and, even when it is achieved, the present distribution of assets and opportunities means that large numbers of poor people are likely to increase their purchasing power only slowly. This report deals with how the second difficulty can be addressed, at least in part, through food and agricultural policies.

The issue of food security has long been a centerpiece of discussions of food and agricultural policy. Many governments feel strongly about this issue and will continue to commit significant amounts of their resources to help alleviate food insecurity. Some of the programs that result are effective and contribute to general economic growth while at the same time providing the poor and disadvantaged with greater access to food. Other programs sacrifice too many of the resources needed for economic growth or fail to reach those whose food security is at stake.

Programs must be tailored to the needs of each country, and, to avoid waste, the cost-effectiveness of alternatives must be carefully evaluated before resources are committed. Ultimately, a careful balancing of measures for trade, production, and poverty alleviation are required in most countries.

There is no one optimal solution to the problem of food security, any more than there is one solution to the problem of poverty. But to help developing countries improve their food security, the international community should:

• Intensify efforts to accelerate growth, through adjustment assistance, policy reform, and productive investment

- Further increase the attention given to poverty alleviation
- Help design, for the short and medium term, cost-effective programs to alleviate chronic hunger and prevent famines, and pay special attention to the needs of the very young, among whom malnutrition can cause irreversible damage
- Help countries coordinate food aid with other forms of economic assistance.

This report outlines the nature and extent of food security problems in developing countries, explores the policy options available to these countries in addressing these problems, and indicates what international institutions such as the World Bank can and should do to help countries solve their food security problems. It suggests policies to achieve the desired goal in cost-effective ways. It also identifies policies that waste economic resources and fail to reach the target groups. It is in that sense as much about what should not be done as about what should be done.

Probably no nation can be 100 percent food secure. That is all the more reason why resources used in the name of food security should be used in cost-effective ways. Each country has to decide how much food security it wants and how many resources it can dedicate to that purpose. This report provides insights and tools for analyzing problems of food security and for designing programs to increase it.

The World Bank stands ready to help countries address their food security problems. It is also prepared to contribute resources. The alleviation of poverty and hunger are, after all, the primary purposes of economic development.

February 1986

A. W. Clausen
President
The World Bank

The report was prepared by Shlomo Reutlinger and Jack van Holst Pellekaan with the assistance of Craig Lissner, Claudia Pendred, and Colleen Roberts. The authors acknowledge the invaluable assistance of Herman van der Tak, Marcelo Selowsky, Hans Binswanger, and G. Edward Schuh in the drafting of the final version. Thanks go to the many readers inside and outside the Bank who reviewed various drafts, to Helen Claverie and Morissa Young for typing, and to Bruce Ross-Larson for editing. The work was carried out under the general direction of S. Shahid Husain.

Contents

Definitions   ix
Glossary   xi

1. **Overview**   1
   Chronic Food Insecurity   1
   Transitory Food Insecurity   4
   Options for National Policy   6
   The Role of External Assistance   10
   Concluding Comments   12

2. **A Problem of Supply or of Purchasing Power?**   13
   Recent Levels of Supplies and Prices   13
   Future Levels of Supplies and Prices   15
   Chronic Food Insecurity   16
   Transitory Food Insecurity   21

3. **National Measures to Reduce Chronic Food Insecurity**   28
   Overview of Policy Interventions   28
   Increasing the Food Supply   30
   Subsidizing Food Prices   34
   Augmenting Incomes   37
   Interventions in Different Conditions   41

4. **National Measures to Reduce Transitory Food Insecurity**   42
   Stabilizing the Domestic Food Supply   43
   Stabilizing Domestic Demand   47
   Protecting Vulnerable Population Groups   47
   Regional Schemes for Cooperation   48

5. International Support for Food Security — 49
Analysis and Advice 50
External Finance 50
International Trade 53

Annex A. Methodologies — 55
Estimating the Share of the Population with Chronically Inadequate Diets 55
Calculating the Approximate Efficiency of a Price Subsidy on Selected Foods 56

Annex B. Data — 58
The Global Food Supply 58
Terms of Trade 61

Annex C. Econometric Analysis of the Determinants of Food Consumption — 63

References — 67

Definitions

Billion is 1,000 million.

Cereals include wheat, rice, maize, rye, sorghum, millet, barley, oats, and mixed grains. The terms "cereal" and "grain" are used interchangeably in this report.

Coefficients of variation are defined as the standard deviation around the same time trend used for growth rates.

Dollars are U.S. dollars unless otherwise specified.

Growth rates used in this report were computed using the least-squares method. The least-squares growth rate, r, is estimated by fitting a least-squares linear trend line to the logarithmic annual values of the variable in the relevant period. More specifically, the regression equation takes the form of $\log X_t = a + bt + e_t$, where this is equivalent to the logarithmic transformation of the compound growth rate equation, $X_t = X_o (1 + r)^t$. In these equations X_t is the variable, t is time, and $a = \log X_o$ and $b = \log (1 + r)$ are the parameters to be estimated; e_t is the error term. If b^* is the least-squares estimate of b, then the annual average growth rate, r, is obtained as $[\text{antilog}(b^*)] - 1$.

Tons are metric tons.

The country groups used in this report are defined as follows:

- *Developing countries* are divided into: low-income economies, with 1983 gross national product (GNP) per person of less than $400; and middle-income economies, with 1983 GNP per person of $400 or more. Middle-income countries are also divided into oil exporters and oil importers, as identified below.
- *Middle-income oil exporters* comprise Algeria, Angola, Cameroon, People's Republic of the Congo, Ecuador, Arab Republic of Egypt, Gabon, Indonesia, Islamic Republic of Iran, Iraq, Malaysia, Mexico, Nigeria, Peru, Syrian Arab Republic, Trinidad and Tobago, Tunisia, and Venezuela.
- *Middle-income oil importers* comprise all other middle-income developing countries not classified as oil exporters.
- *High-income oil exporters* (not included in developing countries) comprise Bahrain, Brunei, Kuwait, Libya, Oman, Qatar, Saudi Arabia, and United Arab Emirates.
- *Industrial market economies* are the members of the Organisation of Economic Co-operation and Development, apart from Greece, Portugal, and Turkey, which are included among the middle-

income developing economies. This group is commonly referred to in the text as industrial economies or industrial countries.

• *East European Nonmarket Economies* include the following countries: Albania, Bulgaria, Czechoslovakia, German Democratic Republic, Hungary, Poland, Romania, and U.S.S.R. This group is sometimes referred to as nonmarket economies.

• *Sub-Saharan Africa* comprises all thirty-nine developing African countries south of the Sahara, excluding South Africa.

• *Middle East and North Africa* includes Afghanistan, Algeria, Arab Republic of Egypt, Iran, Iraq, Israel, Jordan, Kuwait, Lebanon, Libya, Morocco, Oman, Saudi Arabia, Syrian Arab Republic, Tunisia, Turkey, Yemen Arab Republic, People's Democratic Republic of Yemen, and United Arab Emirates.

• *East Asia and Pacific* comprises all low- and middle-income countries of East and Southeast Asia and the Pacific, east of, and including, Burma, China, and Mongolia.

• *South Asia* includes Bangladesh, Bhutan, India, Nepal, Pakistan, and Sri Lanka.

• *Latin America and the Caribbean* comprises all American and Caribbean countries south of the United States.

Glossary

ASEAN	Association of South East Asian Nations	GDP	Gross domestic product
		GNP	Gross national product
CARE	Cooperative for American Relief Everywhere	IBRD	International Bank for Reconstruction and Development
CFF	Compensatory Finance Facility of the IMF	IFPRI	International Food Policy Research Institute
CGIAR	Consultative Group on International Agricultural Research	IMF	International Monetary Fund
		SDR	Special Drawing Rights
CIAT	Centro Internacional de Agricultura Tropical	UNCTAD	United Nations Conference on Trade and Development
CIF	Cost, insurance, and freight	UNDP	United Nations Development Programme
EC	European Communities		
FAO	Food and Agriculture Organization of the United Nations	UNICEF	United Nations Children's Fund
		USDA	United States Department of Agriculture
FOB	Free on board		
GATT	General Agreement on Tariffs and Trade	WFP	World Food Programme
		WHO	World Health Organization

1
Overview

The world has ample food. The growth of global food production has been faster than the unprecedented population growth of the past forty years. Prices of cereals on world markets have even been falling. Enough food is available so that countries that do not produce all the food they want can import it if they can afford to. Yet many poor countries and hundreds of millions of poor people do not share in this abundance. They suffer from a lack of food security, caused mainly by a lack of purchasing power.

The term, "food security," although interpreted in many ways, is defined here as access by all people at all times to enough food for an active, healthy life. Its essential elements are the availability of food and the ability to acquire it. Food insecurity, in turn, is the lack of access to enough food. There are two kinds of food insecurity: chronic and transitory. Chronic food insecurity is a continuously inadequate diet caused by the inability to acquire food. It affects households that persistently lack the ability either to buy enough food or to produce their own. Transitory food insecurity is a temporary decline in a household's access to enough food. It results from instability in food prices, food production, or household incomes—and in its worst form it produces famine.

Chronic Food Insecurity

How many people do not have enough to eat? Where do they live? How have their numbers and geographical distribution changed?

Data for 1970 and 1980

Between 340 million and 730 million people in the developing countries did not have enough income to obtain enough energy from their diet in 1980. (These estimates exclude China because data are not available.) The estimate of 340 million is based on a minimum calorie standard that would prevent serious health risks and stunted growth in children. If the standard is increased to levels that allow an active working life, however, the estimate rises to 730 million (Figure 1-1). About two-thirds of the undernourished live in South Asia and a fifth in Sub-Saharan Africa (see the map on the following page). In all, four-fifths of the undernourished live in countries with very low average incomes.

If it is assumed that income distributions did not change during the 1970s, the share of people with inadequate diets declined between 1970 and 1980 (Figure 1-2). But this assumption is optimistic and

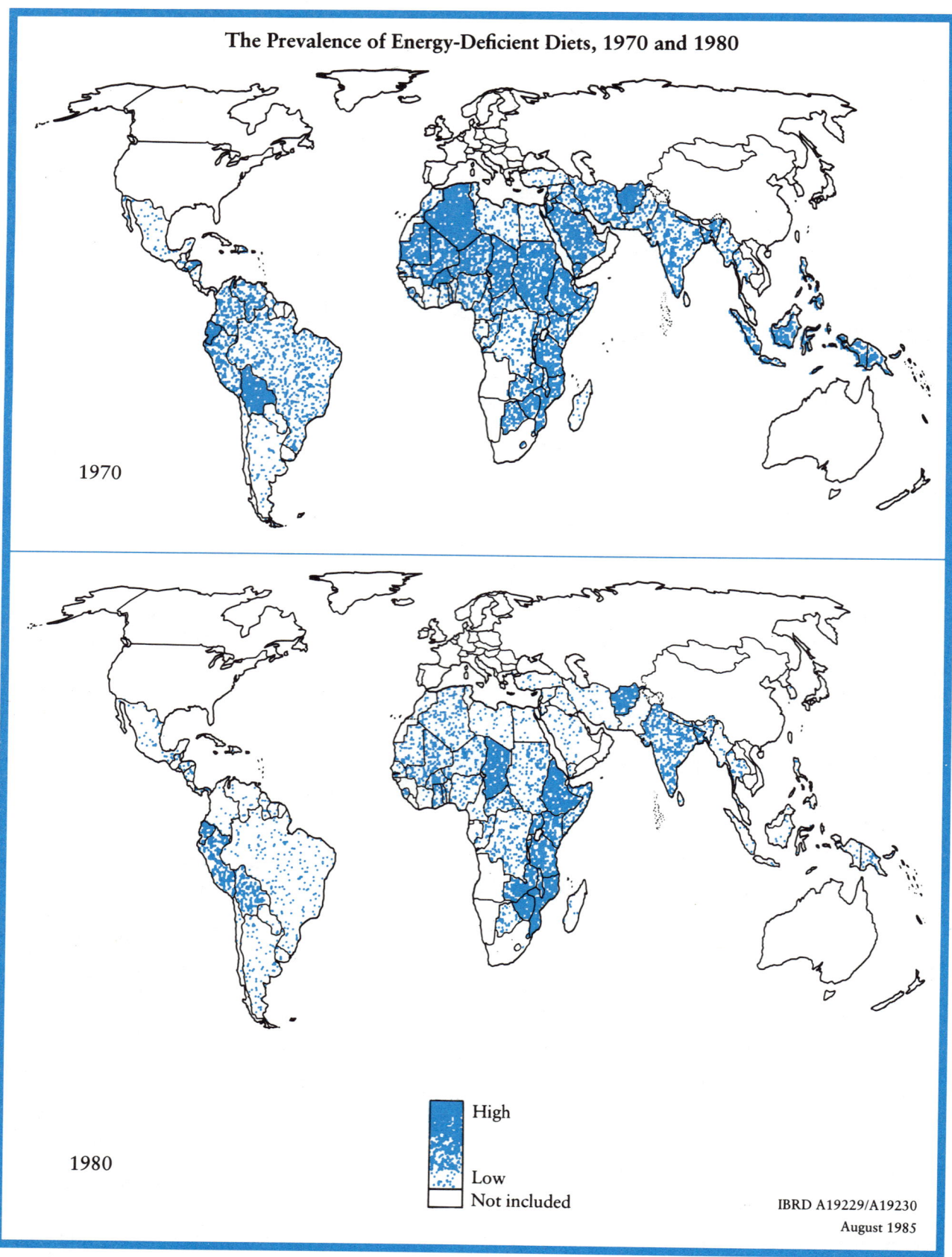

Figure 1-1. The Prevalence of Energy-Deficient Diets in Eighty-seven Developing Countries, 1980

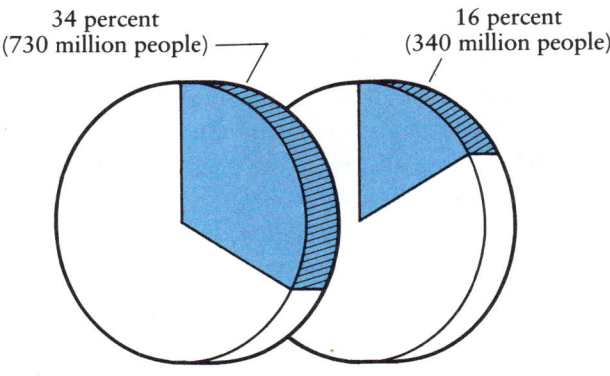
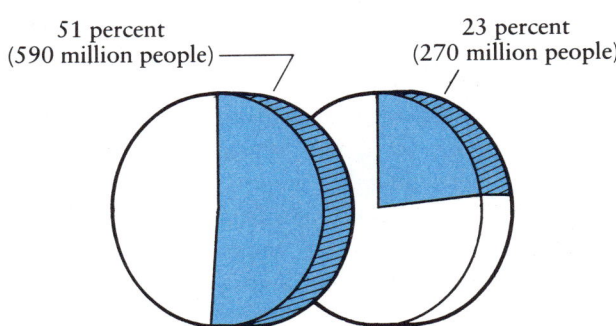
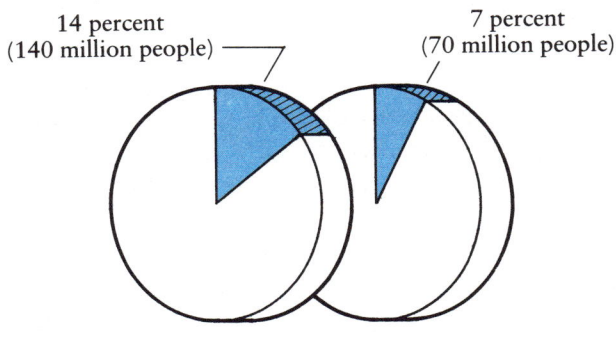

Source: World Bank data.

probably overstates the improvement. In any event, because of population growth, the number of people with inadequate diets appears to have increased under both calorie standards. The largest declines in shares and numbers were in East Asia and the Middle East, regions that enjoyed rapid economic growth during this period. In South Asia and Sub-Saharan Africa, however, the share of the population with deficient diets increased slightly, and the absolute numbers increased markedly.

Income growth was the largest single influence on the dietary improvement between 1970 and 1980. Because average incomes are expected to grow less rapidly, less progress is expected in the 1980s than the 1970s.

Dietary Deficits and Food Supplies

Many people have too little food to sustain an active, healthy life. But the deficiency in their diets represents only a small fraction of the food supply

Figure 1-2. Changes in the Size and Share of Population with Energy-Deficient Diets in Eighty-seven Developing Countries, 1970–80

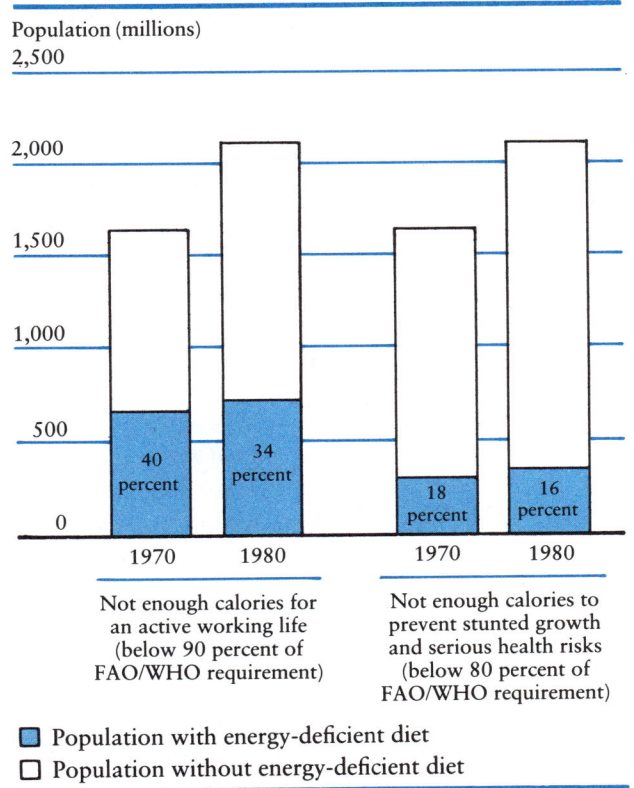

Source: World Bank data.

in most countries—typically less than 5 percent of the national food supply (or possibly 10 percent under the higher standard). This does not mean, however, that a 5 percent increase in food supplies would eliminate malnutrition. It means merely that in many countries the supply of food is not the only obstacle to food security.

In some of the poorest countries, however, the supply of food does need to be greatly increased to reduce chronic food insecurity. When the amount of food consumed by malnourished people is increased through redistributive measures, this increased demand must be added to the already increasing demand caused by population and economic growth. In this situation, the food needs of many nations could not be supplied without significant international assistance for the foreseeable future. Even with unprecedented growth in agricultural production and in export earnings, these countries would still need other sources of finance to import the food they need for food security.

The Costs of Chronic Food Insecurity

The costs of inadequate diets to families and nations are considerable. Inadequate diets increase vulnerability to disease and parasites. They reduce strength for tasks requiring physical effort. They curtail the benefit from schooling and training programs. And they result in a general lack of vigor, alertness, and vitality. These outcomes reduce the productivity of people in the short and long terms, sacrifice output and income, and make it more difficult for families and nations to escape the cycle of poverty.

Transitory Food Insecurity

Because of the lack of data on short-term fluctuations in food consumption, transitory food insecurity has to be assessed by looking at variables that typically influence food consumption. The most important variables are world food prices, domestic food prices, and household purchasing power.

Unstable World and Domestic Prices

Large fluctuations in the international prices of major cereals in 1968–78 illustrate the vulnerability of developing countries to changes in world food markets. The coefficient of variation in prices—one measure of instability and the one used in this report—ranged from about 20 percent for maize to 35 percent for rice. This instability was much greater than that of global production during the same period (Figure 1-3) or of prices in the previous decade.

What then caused this price instability during 1968–78? On the supply side, after years of support programs that created large grain reserves, the large exporters deliberately reduced stocks. This action lowered the proportion of stocks to total consumption and thus caused prices to be more sensitive to fluctuations in production. In addition, demand became more unstable as a result of the sharp rise and subsequent fall in the growth of per capita income in developed and developing market economies, volatile exchange rates, the increasing pursuit of policies that stabilized domestic prices irrespective of international price fluctuations, and new policies in centrally planned economies to use imports to offset sharp fluctuations in their food production. Although price instability in world grain markets is unlikely to be as great as in 1968–78, it continues because many of the same forces that caused past price upheavals still operate.

The supply of food in a country is often strongly influenced by variations in domestic production. With few exceptions, the output of major staple foods has been unstable in developing countries. Consider the differences in variation of the global production of major staple foods and of domestic production by developing countries during 1968–78. On average, the coefficients of variation in eighteen developing countries were 18 percent for wheat production, 14 percent for maize, and 8 percent for rice; globally, the respective coefficients were 5, 4, and 3 percent.

Although developing countries might offset shortfalls in domestic output by importing food, they are often constrained by a shortage of foreign exchange. Their capability to import food has been highly volatile. During 1968–78, the average coefficient of variation in export earnings was about 15 percent for developing countries, compared with about 10 percent for industrial countries. In addition, prior claims for debt repayment and fuel imports and tight foreign exchange reserves limited their ability to offset fluctuations in earnings. As a result, few developing countries have been able to

Figure 1-3. World Prices and Production of Wheat, Rice, and Maize, 1960–84

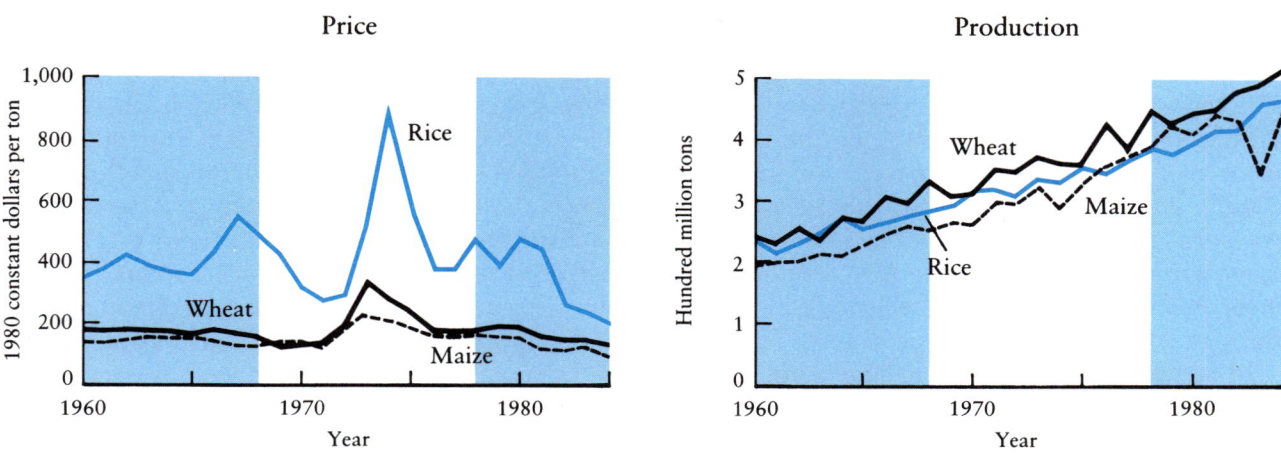

Source: World Bank data.

stabilize domestic food prices as much as have industrial countries that import food. Taking the producer price of wheat in 1968–78 as an example, the average coefficient of variation for eleven industrial countries was 5 percent; for eighteen developing countries it was 12 percent.

Household Purchasing Power

Incomes and food production vary more within households and regions than within countries. In India in 1968–70, for example, aggregate income, food production, and food consumption were fairly stable. Yet survey data of the per capita income and spending of 4,000 rural households showed considerable instability from year to year. Nearly half the households had at least one year in which their per capita income fell below 70 percent of their three-year average. In about two-fifths of the households, total spending and spending on food showed similar deviations from the average.

Famines

Famines, the worst form of transitory food insecurity, can have several causes: wars, floods, crop failures, the loss of purchasing power by groups of households, and—sometimes but not always—high food prices. A decline in the availability of food is not necessarily a primary cause of famines, as research on four particularly disastrous famines has clearly shown. Indeed, by paying too much attention to changes in food availability, governments and relief organizations have sometimes failed to recognize other causes of famines. As a result, some relief has been misdirected.

The loss of real income better explains why famines occur and who is hurt by them. The victims typically belong to one or several groups: small-scale farmers or tenants whose crops have failed and who cannot find other employment, landless agricultural workers who lose their jobs when agricultural production declines or who face a rapid rise in food prices when their wages are stagnant or falling, other rural workers who are affected by a drop in real income in the famine regions, and pastoralists who get most of their food by selling their animals. Problems of supply, such as those in wartime, can aggravate a famine. But famines strike even when foodgrain markets are working well. In several famines, local food prices barely rose, and food was continuously available at those prices. But the victims could not buy it, for they did not have the purchasing power. This underlines the need to focus relief work on those who suffer a fall in real income.

Options for National Policy

The causes of food insecurity suggest that it can be tackled in the long term only by raising the real income of households so that they can afford to acquire enough food. This must be done in two ways: by giving the people who face chronic food insecurity the opportunity to earn an adequate income and by ensuring an adequate food supply through domestic production or imports.

In some countries in which large numbers of people suffer from food insecurity and in which agriculture is the main component of the economy (such as many African countries, India, Bangladesh, and Pakistan), accelerating the growth of agriculture will contribute to both parts of the solution. In fact, any neglect of agriculture in these cases will jeopardize overall economic development—and with it the possibility of providing enough work for the growing population and enough food for all households.

Any policies that raise the incomes of the poor and increase economic growth should obviously be given high priority, since they can reduce or even eradicate chronic food insecurity at no added cost to the economy. Such policies may involve shifting resources from large to small farms, from industry to agriculture, or from capital-intensive activities to labor-intensive activities. They may also involve removing price and trade interventions that reduce incentives to farmers.

But economies cannot be expected to grow quickly enough to eliminate the chronic food insecurity of some groups in the near future, even under the best of circumstances. Moreover, long-run economic growth is often slowed by widespread chronic food insecurity. People who lack energy are ill-equipped to take advantage of opportunities for increasing their productivity and output. That is why policymakers in some countries may want to consider interventions that can speed up food security for the groups worst affected without waiting for the general effect of long-run growth.

The objective of this report is to identify cost-effective ways to increase food security in the short and medium term. Some measures in some circumstances are fully compatible with efficient economic growth. Others involve some tradeoff. Cost-effective measures can minimize this tradeoff. Many national governments place high priority on addressing both chronic and transitory food insecurity. But they often use measures that work against economic growth and food security in the long run. Such measures include persistently overvaluing currencies, spending large sums on consumer food subsidies, and building costly storage facilities to hold excessive stocks of foodgrain. These measures often result in economic waste, draw resources away from more productive activities, slow economic growth, and thus aggravate rather than alleviate long-term food insecurity.

Reducing Chronic Food Insecurity

Beyond the normal array of measures to accelerate economic growth and employment, chronic food insecurity can be addressed by special interventions. These interventions include increasing the food supply (through production or imports), subsidizing consumer prices, and targeting income transfers. Many present macroeconomic adjustment programs increase the price of traded goods (including food) and reduce government expenditure (particularly subsidies). This makes it especially important that interventions to increase food security be cost-effective.

INCREASING THE FOOD SUPPLY. The fundamental question about policies to increase the national supply of food (production plus imports) is this: do they increase the real income and food consumption of the people facing food insecurity? The answer turns on how these policies affect food prices and nominal incomes.

In discussing this question, it is important to distinguish between foods that are internationally traded and foods that are not. The domestic prices of traded foods are determined by world prices, independent of the amounts produced domestically (except insofar as the production of any tradable commodity affects the exchange rate). The prices of nontraded foods are determined by the amounts produced domestically and the effective demand.

The supply of traded foods can be increased only by deliberate measures to increase imports or restrict exports. Increasing the supply of a traded food will tend to lower its domestic price and decrease its domestic production. The effect of the change in the price on the real income of poor people hinges on whether such people are net buyers or net sellers of the food. For net buyers, a fall in the price is unambiguously beneficial: they can afford more of the food and are encouraged to buy more because it is cheaper. These benefits can be considerable, since the poor typically spend one-half to three-quarters of their income on food and only slightly less on basic staples. For net sellers of food, however, a fall in the price of food means a fall in their real income. If the net sellers of food are low-income farmers, they will suffer more food insecurity. If the poor are primarily subsistence farmers—that is, they are neither net buyers nor net sellers—an increase in the supply of a traded food will have little immediate effect on them.

An increase in the domestic production of a traded food will not affect its price. The increases in production will be offset by fewer imports or more exports. Consumers do not gain. The sole beneficiaries will be the farmers producing more food, who may or may not be poor and food insecure.

The supply of nontraded foods obviously can be increased only by increasing domestic production. An increase in the production of a nontraded food will therefore increase its supply and reduce its price. The net buyers of the food will definitely gain. Net sellers of the food, however, might gain or lose, depending on how much the lower price is offset by increased sales and lower production costs.

Thus, the choice of food supply policies should be guided by the characteristics of each commodity and the circumstances of each country. If the poor are primarily net buyers of food—as in countries with widespread urban poverty or a high proportion of rural landless—increasing national food supplies and lowering food prices is an effective policy option. If the poor are primarily net sellers of food—as in Bangladesh and many Sub-Saharan African countries—food security can be increased by reducing the supply of some traded foods and raising their prices and by substituting domestic production for imports. Subsistence farmers will be unaffected. Whatever supply policy is chosen to improve food security is likely to leave some groups of poor people worse off as a result.

Policies directed toward national self-sufficiency in food do not necessarily reduce chronic food insecurity. Self-sufficiency may be associated with a high or low level of food security, depending on its effect on food prices, on the incomes of the poor, and on the availability of food to disadvantaged groups. This conclusion is supported by a statistical analysis of the relation between self-sufficiency in cereals and per capita food consumption in fifty countries. In general, the choice between getting food through added domestic production or through imports should depend on the reliability of alternative food supplies, the comparative advantage of the country in international trade, and the cost of foreign exchange.

SUBSIDIZING FOOD PRICES TO CONSUMERS. A general price subsidy that reduces the consumer price of staple foods while maintaining higher producer prices can sustain the incentives to produce these foods. Such subsidies usually are feasible only if the foods are consumed in processed form and can be centrally processed (such as flour, bread, or tortillas). Otherwise, food will be bought at the low subsidized price and resold at the higher producer price.

Because general price subsidies transfer income to everyone, however, their fiscal cost is high. Although food subsidies usually tend to benefit the poor more than the rich in a relative sense, the income transfers to upper-income groups are sometimes greater than those to disadvantaged groups. Therefore, food price subsidies should be restricted to isolated areas in which the poor are concentrated and to foods that figure heavily in their spending. Moreover, the price should not be so low that the processed food is used to feed livestock or distill alcohol—or is transferred to unintended consumers.

TRANSFERRING INCOME IN CASH AND IN KIND. Transfer payments in cash or in kind tend to be the most efficient way of increasing the real incomes of the poor and of giving them the means to increase their food consumption. A well-known way to transfer income is to ration food to a target group at below-market prices through "fair-price shops" or at no charge through health centers. Such interventions aid mostly urban dwellers and households that normally buy their food or have easy access to such centers. But income could also be transferred to rural households—either in cash or in subsidized rations of consumption goods or farm inputs. The difficulty with this form of intervention lies in avoiding leakage of the transfer payments to unintended beneficiaries. Efforts to target the benefits more sharply to the poor will reduce the fiscal cost of the transfers but will raise—often steeply—the administrative costs and skills required.

Some governments have tried to raise the incomes of the poorest people through public employment programs. These programs seem attractive because only the poorest and the most frequently unemployed are targeted for jobs. But such programs are sometimes inefficient at transferring income to the poor for two reasons. First, they may convey little additional income to workers if the wage offered is only slightly higher than the opportunity wage (whatever they could obtain elsewhere) and if the workers have extra travel costs. Second, the projects may create assets whose value is much lower than the cost of producing them. Together, these two factors can make it expensive to transfer income to the intended beneficiaries.

Employment programs might be more cost-effective if they are used during periods of seasonal food insecurity, when the opportunity wage is very low. It may often be more cost-effective to subsidize private employment or inputs to poor farmers than to initiate public employment schemes. Tax concessions to an industry that uses labor-intensive technologies to produce goods with an elastic demand can go far to improve employment opportunities and thus to increase incomes and food security. A range of options for interventions not necessarily related directly to the food sector is usually available.

COMPARING COST-EFFECTIVENESS. When analyzing the cost-effectiveness of interventions, it is necessary to distinguish between economic costs, budget costs, and income transfers (Figure 1-4). The economic cost consists primarily of the value of resources lost in transferring the income. These involve either delivery costs or efficiency losses. Calculating the delivery costs for explicit income transfers is straightforward. In a food ration program, it is the cost of identifying and certifying the eligible beneficiaries and delivering the subsidized rations. In a program of marketwide subsidies on consumer food prices, it is the excess marketing cost of buying and selling the food. Calculating the efficiency loss of a policy that depresses food prices paid to producers is more difficult. It is the cost of diverting resources from the production of food to the production of commodities of lower value. In each case, calculations are needed to determine whether the delivery costs are higher for targeted or for marketwide interventions and how that cost compares with the efficiency loss from a policy that distorts producer prices. Although the delivery costs come directly from the government budget, the efficiency losses usually are not visible.

Income transfers are not true economic costs. But when directly paid by the government (rather than shifted, say, to farmers through lower input prices), they comprise a large part of the budget cost. Budget costs alone do not measure the size of transfers or the economic costs. Yet they are crucial factors in choosing policy packages. Reducing the budgetary burden of food security interventions can be done in two ways. One is to reduce the income transfer by reducing the number of beneficiaries or the size of the transfer. The second is to shift the cost of the transfer to food producers. The problem with the second way is that it results in efficiency losses.

The choice of interventions needs to be based on a balanced concern for budgetary and economic costs, the administrative and political feasibility of different interventions, and the expected benefits from the interventions. For instance, targeted

Figure 1-4. The Elements of Cost-Effectiveness

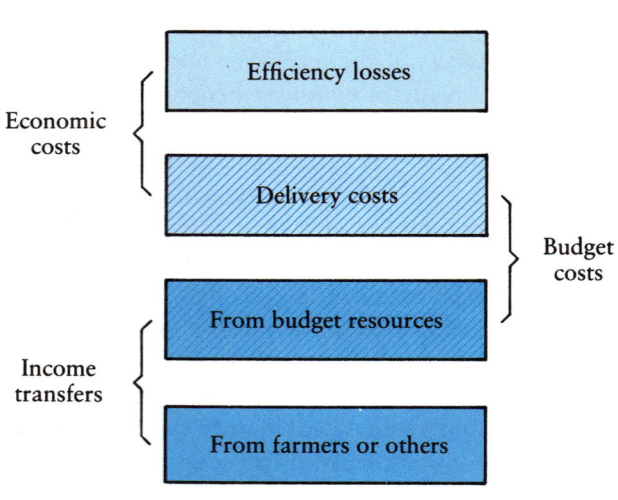

income transfers are surely less burdensome for governments' budgets than marketwide food subsidies, mainly because they do not transfer income to the whole population. But they may be a bureaucratic nightmare and elicit little political support. Similarly, excessive concern with the budgetary implications of interventions may lead governments to favor supply interventions that shift the burden to food producers. But the invisible economic costs of such interventions can be high.

CHOOSING POLICY PACKAGES. Cost-effectiveness is not the only criterion for selecting appropriate interventions. Attention must also be given to the size and makeup of the target population, the government's ability to administer and finance interventions from its budget, and the political feasibility of different interventions.

Most countries have a variety of target groups and thus need a package of measures to improve food security. The appropriateness of the package depends on which groups are facing food insecurity in a country. In several countries in Sub-Saharan Africa, those facing food insecurity are largely food sellers, but they also include some urban poor and rural landless. In these cases, an effective policy package to increase food security is likely to focus on raising producer prices (especially when they are below border prices), on providing subsidies for the urban poor, and possibly on introducing employment programs for the landless. The choice of compensatory policies to protect the net buyers of food will depend on the budgetary cost and administrative requirements of these different options.

If, however, most of those facing food insecurity are urban poor, as in some Latin American countries, measures should be directed mainly at lowering food prices for this target group. Consumer subsidy programs that do not lower prices to producers, such as those that are targeted or that subsidize centrally processed foods, can be cost-effective if they have low budgetary and administrative costs. Otherwise, import prices on selected foods heavily consumed by the poor can be lowered. This would reduce the income of the domestic producers, however, unless they are given compensatory input subsidies.

If those facing food insecurity include many rural landless, subsistence farmers, and urban poor—as is typical in India and Bangladesh—a more complex policy package is needed. It might combine employment programs for the landless, subsidized inputs and infrastructure for subsistence farmers, and targeted food programs for the urban poor. If adequate targeting is not feasible or if budgetary costs are too high, the prices of some staple foods might be lowered through import or production subsidies. But the costs to the budget and to resource efficiency should be kept in mind.

In summary, the choice of measures to address chronic food insecurity involves considerations of the tradeoffs between:
- Sharply targeted interventions, which have high delivery costs but relatively lower budgetary costs
- General consumer subsidies, which are easier to implement and do not distort producer prices but have high budgetary costs
- Import subsidies, which are easy to implement and have low budgetary costs, but distort producer prices and therefore may have large efficiency losses.

The appropriate mix has to be determined for each country because the tradeoffs differ in different circumstances. For marketwide interventions, there is always the danger that political pressures for subsidies will increase after they are introduced. The government then gets locked into burgeoning budget allocations that are difficult to control or phase out.

Reducing Transitory Food Insecurity

Governments that do not prevent transitory food insecurity and food price instability may run significant risks. They may prolong human suffering, lose the human energies essential for development, and disrupt the political fabric of their society. They can reduce such risks by implementing policies that promote stability in the domestic supply and price of staple foods and that provide vulnerable groups with the means to buy enough food as the need arises. These policies—like those for reducing chronic food insecurity—must be determined by the expected costs and benefits.

STABILIZING SUPPLIES AND PRICES. In most countries, the surest and probably the cheapest way to stabilize prices is through international trade. Imports or exports can offset instability in domestic production almost automatically. By using variable levies on externally traded foods, for example, domestic food prices can be insulated from changing international prices. But such policies can wreak havoc with the budget and the balance of payments unless governments hold larger reserves of foreign exchange and rely more on food aid or international insurance schemes for financing variable food imports, such as the expanded Compensatory Financing Facility of the International Monetary Fund.

Governments trying to stabilize food supplies and prices often do so in costly and ineffective ways. They use quantitative controls on imports and exports of foods—controls that require substantially more information on supply and demand than public marketing agencies typically have. Even when this information is available, the agencies seldom have the managerial resources or the political support to act promptly and effectively. As a result, government interventions often aggravate rather than reduce the instability of supply and prices.

Some governments keep excessive buffer stocks. Large stocks are seldom cost-effective because of high storage losses, low capacity utilization of storage facilities, and high interest charges on capital tied up in inventory. Countries with access to foreign exchange usually find it cheaper to stabilize prices by varying their exports and imports rather than by using buffer stocks, even if world market prices are unstable. Storage costs are usually far greater than the cost of borrowing or of carrying extra reserves so as to be able to import more when the occasion demands. When food supplies cannot be stabilized through trade, investing in measures to stabilize production, such as irrigation or pest control, or to improve the efficiency of domestic marketing is sometimes less costly than relying on buffer stocks.

PREPARING FOR PRECIPITATE DECLINES IN SUPPLY. Countries might stabilize supplies by adjusting their food trade but might lack the capability to make the food available where and when it is needed. To overcome this, countries should invest in speeding their response time by means such as better early warning systems, faster orders for additional shipments, and speedier internal movements of supplies. If response times cannot be improved, small emergency food stocks may be needed in strategic places to bridge the gap until added deliveries can be made.

ASSISTING VULNERABLE GROUPS DIRECTLY. Stable food prices and efficient domestic marketing are not always enough to prevent transitory food insecurity and certainly cannot prevent famines. Even if markets are working perfectly, the most severely affected groups can still lack the purchasing power to buy food. Such groups include the rural landless whose employment and wages are severely depressed, the small-scale farmer or herder whose marketable surplus has been destroyed or who faces adverse terms of trade, and the artisan or urban worker whose opportunities for work have collapsed. These groups must be identified quickly and provided with income in cash or in kind. If a country can administer cost-effective work programs, these groups must be given temporary employment. And if resources are severely limited, special programs should at least preserve the nutrition of children under five and of pregnant and lactating women.

The Role of External Assistance

So far, much of the foreign assistance for food security has sought to accelerate agricultural development and increase food production. These are important aspects of the problem, especially when they affect the real incomes of vulnerable consumers and producers. But there has been only modest progress in diminishing worldwide food insecurity, partly because of the widely held misperception that food shortages are the root of the problem. The disturbing fact is that food security problems have become more serious in many countries. Food insecurity remains even in countries that have high per capita food production.

The international community, in supporting food security, should take into account the four most important conclusions of this report:

• The lack of food security is a lack of purchasing power of people and nations. Thus, there is a strong convergence between the objectives of alleviating poverty and ensuring food security.

• Food security does not necessarily come from achieving food self-sufficiency in a country, nor from a rapid increase in food production.

• Food security in the long run is a matter of achieving economic growth and alleviating poverty. But food security in the shorter run means achieving a redistribution of purchasing power and resources. By choosing redistributive policies that are also cost-effective, governments can do much to reduce the costs of improving the food security of their people.

• Transitory food insecurity linked to fluctuations in domestic harvests, international prices, and foreign exchange earnings can best be reduced through measures that facilitate trade and provide income relief to afflicted people.

International donors can help nations apply these conclusions to their food security strategies in three ways: by helping to identify and formulate appropriate policies to alleviate food insecurity, by providing finance to support these policies, and by improving the external trading environment.

Policy Advice

National policies have the greatest influence on the food security of countries. The main objective of external advice should be to help countries pursue cost-effective food security interventions, which take into account budgetary, political, and administrative constraints.

The international community should help countries to assess food security problems and to develop the analytical capability to formulate remedial policies. The assessments should always clearly differentiate between chronic and transitory food insecurity and should identify the size and characteristics of the vulnerable groups and the sources of instability in food production, prices, and incomes.

External Finance

Efforts to support food security in line with the remedies advocated in this report should proceed in three directions. The first is to continue to emphasize lending operations that benefit the poorest people. The second is to increase the use of trade finance and other international financing arrangements to provide resources for alleviating transitory food insecurity. The third is to integrate food aid with financial aid.

Several recommendations for providing external financing can be made.

• Lending operations that support policy adjustments needed for faster economic growth should consider the implications of the reforms for food security. When necessary, adjustment programs should include cost-effective programs to safeguard the food security of the people most vulnerable, particularly lactating women and children under five.

• Projects should continue to emphasize investments that benefit the poorest people. This includes, where appropriate, financing investments that increase the supply and reduce the price of basic staple foods. External finance should also continue to be allocated for cost-effective programs to improve the nutrition of vulnerable groups through income transfers, nutrition education, drinking water supply, preventive health services, and means for family planning.

• External finance should help countries improve their capacity to handle sharp, sporadic increases in food imports and intraregional food transfers that may be needed from time to time to ensure food security. It should also help the countries to establish small, strategically located emergency stocks to tide them over while awaiting additional imports.

• In climatically unstable regions, external finance should support projects that include components—such as crop diversification, public employment, and transport facilities—to help sustain minimally adequate food consumption in years of adverse weather conditions.

• Donors of food aid should coordinate their efforts with other development institutions to improve the effectiveness of external assistance.

• To improve the cost-effectiveness of food aid provided directly to poor households, foods should have a high value to the recipients relative to the delivered costs. Exchanging donated food for cash and buying local foods may often be more advantageous to recipients.

• The cost-effectiveness of famine relief should be improved by detecting emergencies earlier, reducing the response time, and providing aid in cash as well as food.

• Food aid should be administered so that it can effectively alleviate transitory food insecurity of all kinds, including that caused by high international food prices. Food aid budgets in 1985 were quite responsive to the crisis in Africa. In general, however, food aid budgets tend to be fixed from one year to the next; as a result, when prices rise, less food can be bought. Even worse, food aid budgets are often curtailed when prospects for commercial exports improve. Multiyear commitments by food aid donors, with flexible drawings against those commitments in accord with the needs of recipient countries, are required.

International Trade

The terms of trade for commodities greatly affect the real income of vulnerable groups, primarily through effects on food prices and on the earnings of these groups. International concern for food security should therefore be translated into a concern for how the policies of developed countries limit international trading opportunities. Multilateral and bilateral actions to reduce trade restrictions on the exports of developing countries would help most, since the poor often work in the labor-intensive production of export goods. Moreover, trade restrictions cause international markets to be more unstable than they would be otherwise, and thus contribute to transitory food insecurity. Actions that stabilize food prices and major exchange rates would help as well. The international community could also provide technical assistance to help developing countries use the same tools that developed countries use to manage trade risks.

Concluding Comments

Many countries have intervened in their economies in the name of food security. In some cases, however, these interventions have incurred high costs in terms of sacrificed economic growth. Policymakers need to be sensitive to these costs and to the difficulties of reducing or eliminating interventions once they are in place. Three key issues need to be kept in mind:

- Interventions to improve food security have both costs and benefits
- Some forms of intervention are more cost-effective than others, and these cost-effective measures should be chosen
- Costs and benefits should be calculated in the context of each individual economy.

2

A Problem of Supply or of Purchasing Power?

Food is abundant worldwide, and nations with the means to buy it have no problem acquiring all they need. But anxiety about food supplies remains high in many countries—and this worry has led some governments to devote substantial resources to increasing food production. Preoccupation with food production is misguided, however, when it takes priority over more immediate concerns. One such concern is that many poor countries—and hundreds of millions of poor people—cannot get even a modest share of the world's abundant food supply. In response to this concern, this report focuses on the food insecurity that arises from the inadequate purchasing power of households and nations. This emphasis does not mean that promoting food production and improving food trade are unimportant; it means that an adequate income is essential for ensuring food security.

The term "food security" came into use about ten years ago to describe a broad range of development issues. It is perhaps natural to put new labels on old problems that defy easy solutions, but the price of combining loosely related subjects under a new name can be high. For example, redefining problems of agricultural development and general development as problems of food security does little to increase understanding of either issue.

This chapter assesses whether food insecurity is an issue of food supply or an issue of poverty—whether it is the outcome of inadequate food supplies or inadequate purchasing power. Evidence on food supplies and prices in the 1970s shows that there was enough food for all the world's people. Projections to 2000 indicate that world food production is likely to keep pace with effective global demand, perhaps even at a lower price (although debt-ridden countries may find that domestic food prices will go up because of scarce foreign exchange). Why, then, do both chronic and transitory food insecurity persist? An analysis of the causes of food insecurity concludes that the main cause is not lack of supply or even high prices. The main cause is the weak purchasing power of some households and nations. This conclusion, along with the sharp distinction between chronic and transitory food insecurity, sets the stage for the analysis of national and international policy issues in later chapters.

Recent Levels of Supplies and Prices

The growth in global grain production has more than kept pace with the growth in population (Table 2-1). In fact, grain output increased faster than population during the 1970s for developing countries as a group, but not in Eastern Europe, the Middle East, or Sub-Saharan Africa. Data on grains are used to indicate the total supply of food

13

Table 2-1. Grain Production and Population Growth, by Country Group, 1970–82

Country group or region	Cereal production	Population	Cereal production per capita
World	2.3	1.8	0.5
Industrial market economies	2.3	0.7	1.6
East European nonmarket economies	0.6	0.8	−0.2
Developing economies	3.0	2.1	0.9
East Africa	0.8	3.0	−2.2
West Africa	1.9	2.7	−0.8
East Asia and Pacific	3.5	1.7	1.8
South Asia	2.7	2.4	0.3
Middle East and North Africa	1.7	2.9	−1.2
Latin America and the Caribbean	3.2	2.4	0.8

Average annual percentage change

Note: The term "grain" includes wheat, rice, maize, rye, sorghum, millet, barley, oats, and mixed grains. All growth rates in all tables have been computed using the least-squares method.
Source: World Bank calculations based on USDA data.

because data for other foods are less reliable and because grain is the most commonly consumed food in developing countries. In Sub-Saharan Africa, however, root crops are often just as important as grains in people's diets. Even when production estimates for root crops are included with grains, per capita food output is still shown to have declined (see Table B-1 in Annex B).

Trends in per capita food production are not, however, a good measure of food scarcity in countries. Because the global and domestic food markets are increasingly integrated, the trend in world grain prices emerges as a better measure for judging the availability of food. Together with trends in the scarcity of foreign exchange, it determines the true costs of food to nations and consumers.

For decades, the real dollar prices for grains in the world market—defined as crop-year average prices deflated by the 1980 U.S. consumer price index—have declined (Figure 2-1). Prices did rise sharply above the long-run trend in the early 1970s, but, in real terms, wheat prices now are about 15 percent below the level of the early 1970s and 20 percent below the level of the 1960s. Maize prices declined even more. Although rice prices rose in the early 1970s, they also have been falling during the past six years and are projected to continue to do so (World Bank 1984). Of the many factors that influence these price trends, two stand out: rapid improvement in farm production technology and slower growth in effective demand.

Technological improvements have reduced production costs and increased the output of world agriculture, particularly that of the largest cereal-exporting countries. Most technological improvements have been focused on increasing yields and account, during the past twenty years, for about 65 percent of the increase in global rice production, 80 percent of that in wheat, and 90 percent of that in coarse grains. Investment in infrastructure (such as irrigation and transport facilities), remunerative farmgate prices for domestic output, greater access to credit, and improvements in agricultural extension all have made it possible to adopt Green Revolution technology and to boost production in many parts of the world.

The revolution in technology has not, however, affected all crops and regions equally. (Annex B shows the differences in yield increases of the five most important cereals between 1960 and 1982.) For example, the remarkable increases in India, Southeast Asia, and parts of Latin America have not materialized in Africa. Nevertheless, because of the greater integration of international commodity markets in recent years, the technological advances in the major grain-producing countries have kept world grain prices down. These countries can now adjust supplies quickly to shifts in world demand. The shifts in supply have tended to be larger than shifts in demand, which has resulted in the trend of declining prices.

This declining trend in real prices also reflects recent sluggish growth in the demand for cereal—a function of the slower growth of population and per capita incomes. In most countries, the gross domestic product (GDP) grew much slower in the early 1980s than in the 1960s and 1970s (Table 2-2). Annual GDP growth in the middle-income devel-

Figure 2-1. Trends in World Prices of Wheat, Rice, and Maize, 1960–84
(1980 constant dollars)

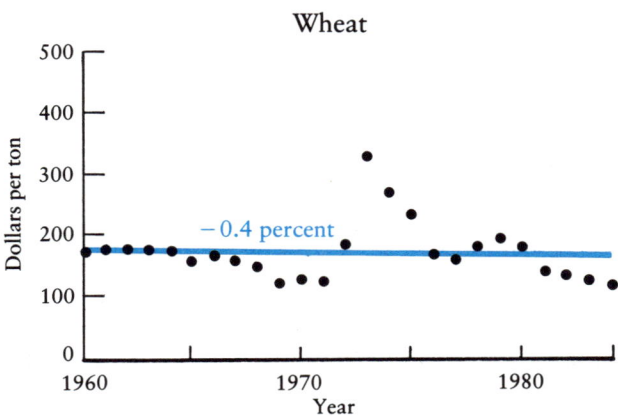

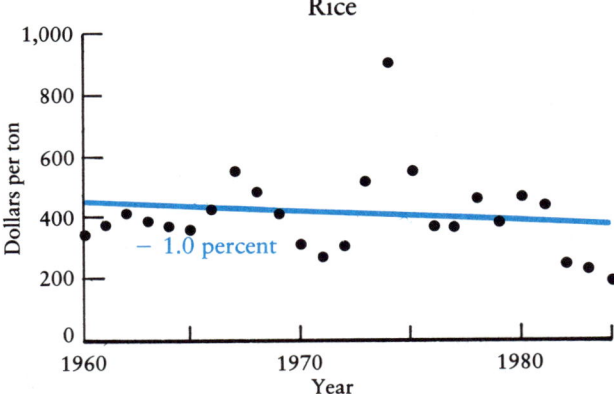

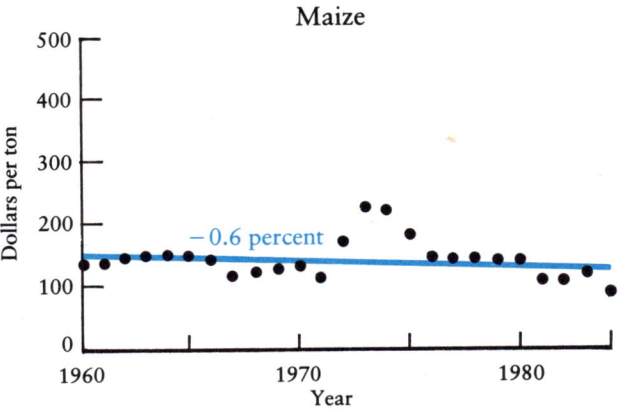

Source: World Bank.

oping countries, which previously had imported large amounts of grain for people and livestock, fell from almost 6 percent in 1973–80 to about 1 percent in 1982–84. Similarly, the growth of GDP in developed countries dropped from 2.8 percent a year during the middle and late 1970s to 1 percent in 1981 and 1982. Simultaneously, purchases by the developed countries of wheat and coarse grains from world markets stagnated and in some cases fell.

Dollar prices in world markets may reliably reflect supply and demand in international markets, but they are not an accurate measure of the price of imported cereals in domestic currency once adjustments are made for exchange rates, domestic inflation, and transport costs. International grain prices have fallen steadily, but the price of imported grain in domestic currencies after adjusting for the exchange rate has not always moved in the same direction. For example, between 1970 and 1983 the real rupee price for Sri Lanka's wheat and rice imports grew more than 7 percent a year while real dollar prices fell about 1.5 percent a year (see Annex B, Table B-2).

Future Levels of Supplies and Prices

Most projections show that global food production will continue to increase fast enough to meet the effective demand generated by growth in population and incomes. This added production will come primarily from better use of resources and improved technology, not from cultivation of more land.

Biogenetic research is under way to produce new crop varieties that require fewer inputs and that tolerate pests, drought, and disease. Years of work in developing hardier and more productive strains of subsistence tropical food crops—yams, beans, millet, sorghum, and cassava—are also beginning to pay off. Current research on the placement and timing of fertilizer applications will increase the efficiency of inputs. Investments in lower-cost, higher-efficiency devices for water control and management (such as small tubewells and irrigation-ditch lining) as well as investments in transport, marketing, and support services are also expected to improve agricultural productivity. As a result, the cost of increasing food production throughout the world should decline, and real world food prices should continue to fall.

Africa's problems and remedies are more complex and controversial than those of other regions,

Table 2-2. Gross Domestic Product, 1980, and Growth Rates, 1965–84, by Country Group

Country group	1980 GDP per capita (dollars)	Average annual percentage change in GDP					
		1965–73	1973–80	1981	1982	1983[a]	1984[b]
Developing countries	670	6.6	5.5	3.3	1.9	2.0	4.1
Low-income countries	260	5.5	4.9	4.0	5.0	7.2	6.6
Middle-income oil importers	1,690	7.0	5.6	2.0	0.8	0.7	3.3
Middle-income oil exporters	1,270	7.1	5.8	4.6	0.9	−1.0	2.7
High-income oil exporters	10,650	9.2	7.7	0.1	−1.7	−7.0	0.6
Industrial market economies	10,420	4.7	2.8	1.4	−0.3	2.3	4.8

a. Estimated.
b. Projected.
Source: World Bank (1985), p. 149.

including Asia in the 1960s. Yet, because of progress in agricultural research, technological constraints can be addressed with more understanding than before. There appears to be a great potential for improving yields in Sub-Saharan Africa, although fragile soils and a variable climate in many areas make it difficult to sustain increased food production, whether under extensive or intensive farming. The costs of increasing food production there will be high unless technology improves considerably. Achieving such improvement will require many years of research.

A few analysts acknowledge that future world supplies of food will meet effective demand but contend that the relative price of food will rise sharply (Brown 1984). They assume that the deterioration of the agricultural resource base will outpace technical change. No doubt, the agricultural base has deteriorated in many parts of the world, and, if unchecked, the deterioration will increase the cost of agricultural production in these areas. Deforestation and soil erosion already are catastrophic in many regions. In the Sahel, for example, an estimated 1 percent of the natural forest cover is lost each year. Despite these losses, pessimism about world food prices is not warranted. Technological developments can help farmers adjust their farming systems to fragile environments. To be sure, changes in institutions, in price and credit policies, and in the distribution of landholdings will be needed in many countries and regions to support technological advances. Many such changes are already taking place and provide solid ground for optimism about the continuing ability of global food supplies to meet demand and hold prices down.

Of course, some uncertainties about supplies persist. The needed policy changes, institutional adjustments, and technological developments may not occur or have the expected effect. In addition, other complicating factors cannot be ignored. For example, a major economic disturbance such as that of the 1930s, with serious distortions of international trade and associated economic collapse, could have a serious effect on both the supply of food and the ability to acquire it.

Another uncertainty is the future price of foreign exchange for individual countries. If it increases, domestic prices could rise and thus reduce the food available to households. Constrained export opportunities, declining terms of trade, and high external debt repayments could combine to make foreign exchange scarcer in developing countries —and increase the cost of food imports in domestic currency, even if world prices continue to fall. Countries short of foreign exchange will then find it advantageous to produce fewer nontradables and more tradables, including many foods.

Chronic Food Insecurity

Just as national per capita income is a poor indicator of the prevalence of poverty, so per capita food consumption is a poor indicator of the number of people consuming inadequate amounts of food. With this in mind, two questions are addressed here: how many people in the developing world do not get enough food to eat, and is their number and share of the total declining or increasing?

What Is an Adequate Diet?

The amount of food (or energy) a person needs is

not easy to determine: social activities, employment, genetically determined differences in the efficiency of food conversion, environmental factors, and individual preferences all come into play. People can survive with barely minimal diets. If the physical effort needed to earn an income is considered, however, the diets of many people are inadequate. And if the energy to grow and take part in social life and economic development is also taken into account, even more people have inadequate diets (Beaton 1983). Even if there were a consensus about what performance criterion should be used, the adequacy of diets is not easily determined. Only if both the energy intake and the energy requirements were known—person by person—could researchers estimate more precisely the prevalence of energy-deficient diets. Such data have never been compiled.

Concern for chronic food insecurity must therefore focus on the adequacy of average food consumption for specific socioeconomic groups. It is possible to estimate the energy deficiency for these groups from the relation between food consumption and income without knowing how intake and requirements vary within the group. For instance, the poorest groups consume less food, contract more diseases, have higher mortality rates, and are more likely to be physically stunted or exert less energy in their daily tasks than the rich. Inadequate food consumption, although only one of many factors that impairs their performance, clearly prevents them from leading productive lives.

The Prevalence of Deficient Diets

Estimates of the prevalence of energy-deficient diets are deduced from data on the energy content of average diets in eighty-seven developing countries in 1980 and data on income distribution patterns in thirty-five countries (Table 2-3). The estimates show, for two standards of energy requirements, the share and number of people with energy-deficient diets in various regions—the people who face chronic food insecurity. If the energy standard adopted is merely enough calories to prevent stunted growth and serious health risks, an estimated 340 million people, or a sixth of the people in eighty-seven developing countries, had energy-deficient diets. If the standard is enough calories for an active working life, some 730 million people, or a third of the people in the same countries, lived with dietary deficits. Most of these people—four out of every five—were in low-income countries. This higher figure is the better guide to the harm that inadequate diets impose on development.

How did chronic food insecurity change during the 1970s? The choice of a standard is not an important issue in this case. Moreover, imprecise estimates of the *level* of chronic food insecurity do

Table 2-3. Prevalence of Energy-Deficient Diets in Eighty-seven Developing Countries, 1980

Country group or region[a]	Not enough calories for an active working life (below 90 percent of FAO/WHO requirement)[b] Share in population (percent)	Population (millions)	Not enough calories to prevent stunted growth and serious health risks (below 80 percent of FAO/WHO requirement)[c] Share in population (percent)	Population (millions)
Developing countries (87)	34	730	16	340
Low-income (30)[d]	51	590	23	270
Middle-income (57)	14	140	7	70
Sub-Saharan Africa (37)	44	150	25	90
East Asia and Pacific (8)	14	40	7	20
South Asia (7)	50	470	21	200
Middle East and North Africa (11)	10	20	4	10
Latin America and the Caribbean (24)	13	50	6	20

a. The eighty-seven countries had 92 percent of the population in developing countries in 1980, excluding China. See Annex A, Table A-1 for regional classification of countries. Numbers in parentheses are the number of countries in the sample.
b. See Annex A for an explanation of FAO/WHO requirements. Intake at this standard is sufficient for a person to function at full capacity in all daily activities.
c. Intake at this standard is sufficient to prevent high health risks and growth retardation in children.
d. The low-income countries had a per capita income below $400 in 1983: the middle-income countries had a per capita income above $400 in 1983.
Source: World Bank estimates.

Table 2-4. Changes in the Prevalence of Energy-Deficient Diets in Eighty-seven Developing Countries, 1970–80

Country group or region	Not enough calories for an active working life (below 90 percent of FAO/WHO requirement)		Not enough calories to prevent stunted growth and serious health risks (below 80 percent of FAO/WHO requirement)	
	Change in share of population	Percentage change in number of people	Change in share of population	Percentage change in number of people
Developing countries (87)	−0.06	+10	−0.02	+14
Low-income (30)	+0.04	+41	+0.03	+54
Middle-income (57)	−0.18	−43	−0.09	−44
Sub-Saharan Africa (37)	+0.01	+30	+0.04	+49
East Asia and Pacific (8)	−0.27	−57	−0.14	−57
South Asia (7)	+0.03	+38	+0.02	+47
Middle East and North Africa (11)	−0.25	−62	−0.14	−68
Latin America and the Caribbean (24)	−0.07	−15	−0.04	−21

Note: See the footnotes to Table 2-3.
Source: World Bank estimates.

not necessarily invalidate estimates of the *changes* in food insecurity.

The *share* of people with deficient diets in the eighty-seven developing countries declined between 1970 and 1980 under both standards of adequacy (Table 2-4). The estimates rest on the rather optimistic assumption that income distribution did not change during the decade; this probably overstates the improvement, as explained in Box 2-1. The sharpest declines were in East Asia and the Middle East, where per capita incomes rose rapidly. The share declined much less in low-income countries than in middle-income countries. In South Asia and Sub-Saharan Africa, however, the share of people with energy-deficient diets increased somewhat.

The *total number* of people with energy-deficient diets has increased under both standards (see Figure 1-2). Compared with 1970, 170 million more people in the low-income countries had deficient diets under the higher standard in 1980—90 million more under the lower standard.

Another way to infer changes in chronic food insecurity is to observe changes in the energy content of national average diets—again assuming that income distribution remained constant. About 770 million people live in countries in which the energy content of the national food consumption was low in 1970 and declined further by 1980 (Figure 2-2).

Prognosis for the Future

Chronic food insecurity, if measured by the *share* of people, is likely to continue to diminish, but if it is measured by the *number* of people, it is likely to continue to increase. Some evidence also suggests that the progress achieved in the 1970s will not be repeated in the 1980s. For instance, the energy content of the average diet in all countries

---

Box 2-1. Income Distribution and Diet

The data necessary to directly measure changes in income distribution generally are not available. The literature suggests, however, that increases in income tend not to be distributed equally during the early stages of development (Kuznets 1975; Ahluwalia 1976; and Chenery and Syrquin 1975). A comparison of rates of change in the energy content of national diets and in per capita income also suggests that the growth of income during the 1970s was not fully shared by low-income people, who need more energy in their daily diet. In Brazil, for instance, per capita income more than doubled while per capita calorie consumption changed little during one decade. To the extent that income distribution becomes more unequal, the estimated size of the population with energy-deficient diets in 1980, shown in Tables 2-3 and 2-4, has been underestimated. Actual changes may have been less favorable.

Figure 2-2. Changes in the Population and in the Energy Content of the Food Consumed in Eighty-seven Developing Countries, 1970–80

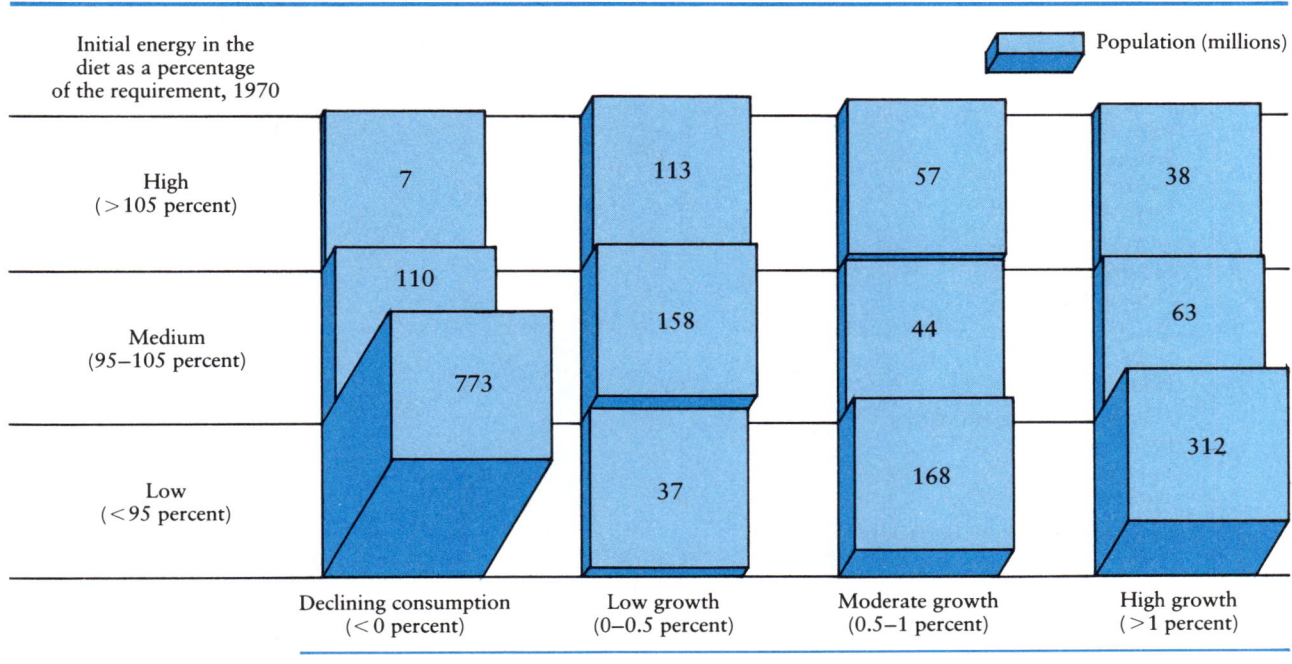

Source: Data from FAO (1977, 1980b).

during the 1970s, weighted for the population, grew 0.4 percent a year—about 100 calories during the decade. This growth was associated with growth in per capita income of 2.6 percent a year. But the growth of per capita income in the 1980s is projected to be less than in the 1970s, and per capita income is the most important determinant of growth in the energy content of national diets. So the decline in the share of people with energy-deficient diets will probably be less in the 1980s than in the 1970s, and, if the population continues to grow at present rates, the number of people facing chronic food insecurity will increase further.

Even a small increase in the energy content of the average national diet—say, 2 percent during the current decade—could reduce the share of people with energy-deficient diets by 10 percent. But this would occur only if the poor shared proportionately in the additional food consumption. The poor, however, tend to bear the brunt of slower or negative growth in per capita income. Moreover, food price subsidies and other government programs to benefit the poor tend to be sharply reduced during hard times.

National Food Deficits

Although many people face food insecurity, the aggregate energy lacking in their diets is only a small part of the energy in the food supply of most nations (Table 2-5). Even under the higher calorie standard, the aggregate energy deficit in most countries is far less than 10 percent of the food supply. For a sample of thirty-five countries, the deficit is 3.5 percent of supply under the higher standard and 0.9 percent under the lower standard. Increasing the food supply by 3.5 percent would not eliminate the energy deficiency, since it would not necessarily improve the incomes and purchasing power of the poor. For most developing countries, the supply of food—even the cost of that food—is not the greatest barrier to achieving national food security. In many countries, the national food supply (domestic production plus imports) is now sufficient or could easily expand to provide the entire population with enough energy if it were distributed more evenly. Nonetheless some low-income countries, particularly in Africa, do have a national supply problem. Even assuming

Table 2-5. Energy Deficit of Energy-Deficient Diets as a Percentage of Energy in the Total Food Supply in Selected Low-Income Countries, 1980
(percent)

Region and country	Not enough calories for an active working life (below 90 percent of FAO/WHO requirement)	Not enough calories to prevent stunted growth and serious health risks (below 80 percent of FAO/WHO requirement)
Sub-Saharan Africa		
Kenya	8.9	3.3
Senegal	2.5	0.9
Sudan	2.5	0.9
Tanzania	7.8	2.8
East Asia and Pacific		
Indonesia	2.0	0.5
Philippines	1.9	0.6
South Asia		
India	5.6	1.4
Pakistan	1.2	0.4
Middle East and North Africa		
Iraq	2.3	0.9
Tunisia	1.0	0.4
Turkey	0.7	0.3
Latin America and the Caribbean		
Brazil	1.3	0.4
Colombia	0.9	0.3
Dominica Republic	3.5	0.9
Ecuador	8.8	3.1
Sample of thirty-five countries[a]	3.5	0.9

a. Countries listed in Annex A, Table A-1.
Source: World Bank estimates.

rapid growth in domestic production, large increases in food imports will be required to meet the needs in those countries.

Given the present food supply in six selected low-income countries, energy consumption would be insufficient to satisfy requirements even if the supplies were evenly distributed among the population (Table 2-6). The food imports required to improve their food security by 1990 have been projected on the following assumptions:

• The energy content of the national food supply is set at 100 percent of the FAO/WHO requirement to ensure an adequate diet for all groups in the population. This takes into account the wide

Table 2-6. Volume of Cereal Imports and Their Value as a Share of Export Earnings for Selected Low-Income Countries

Country[a]	Food production (thousands of tons)[b] 1978–80[d]	1990	Cereal imports (thousands of tons) 1978–80[d]	1990	Cost of cereal imports as a proportion of export earnings[c] 1978–80[d]	1990
Burkina Faso (85)	1,221	1,690	52	250	0.06	0.19
Ethiopia (74)	5,307	7,346	214	3,061	0.08	0.86
Mali (85)	1,293	1,790	65	377	0.06	0.20
Nepal (87)	2,872	3,976	−23	367	−0.02	0.22
Tanzania (87)	3,646	5,048	157	1,306	0.05	0.49
Uganda (80)	2,348	3,251	43	1,073	0.02	0.34

Note: The assumptions needed to derive the numbers in this table are given in the text.
a. Numbers in parentheses are the energy content of average daily diets in 1978–80 as a percentage of the FAO/WHO requirement.
b. Food production figures were derived from estimated food consumption data (FAO 1980b).
c. The FOB cost of cereals is estimated at $200 per metric ton.
d. Annual average.
Sources: Cereal data for 1978–80 from USDA. Export earnings data for 1978–80 and projections for 1990 are from the World Bank. Cereal projections and country export earnings for 1990 are World Bank estimates.

differences in food consumption among people in each country.

- Population will expand at the currently projected rate.
- Food production will grow at the optimistic rate of 3 percent a year (past growth for these countries ranged from −0.1 to 3.2 percent a year).
- Export earnings will grow at rates now projected by the World Bank.

The projections illustrate that high volumes of food imports would be required in 1990 to meet per capita energy requirements—imports these countries cannot afford. In Ethiopia, for instance, the bill for required cereal imports is almost the same as the projected export earnings. If cereal imports are held to 10 percent of their export earnings, international transfer payments such as food aid would have to expand greatly (Figure 2-3). For many of the countries, the transfer would need to grow more than tenfold. Achieving food security in these countries will therefore require a joint commitment of governments and the international community.

Figure 2-3. Average Annual Food Aid, 1978–80, and Projected Food Aid Requirements, 1990, for Six Low-Income Countries

(thousands of tons)

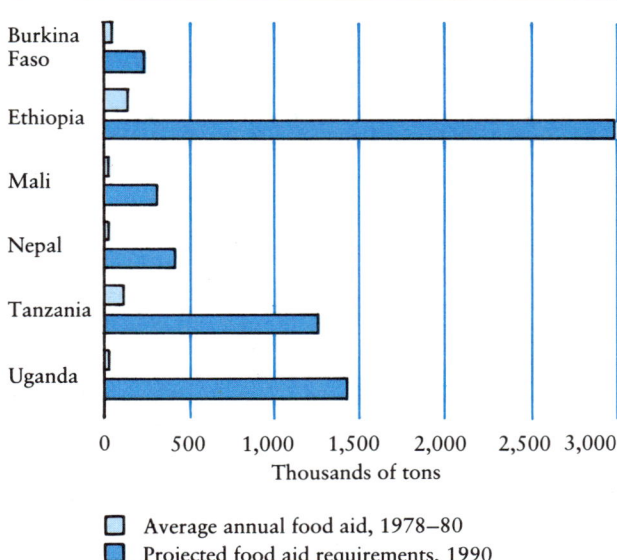

☐ Average annual food aid, 1978–80
■ Projected food aid requirements, 1990

Note: Estimates for 1990 are based on the methodology described in the text.
Source: World Bank estimates.

Food import requirements were projected also for thirty-one developing countries in which conditions are better, and the results are quite different (Figure 2-4). For instance, the six countries will need to import 53 kilograms of cereal per capita in 1990, a ninefold increase over their imports in 1978–80. The thirty-one countries will need barely 12 kilograms per capita in 1990—only twice the imports in 1978–80. The difference in the cost of food imports as a proportion of export earnings is also large between the two groups. If anything, these disparities are understated, since the group of thirty-one countries is more likely than the group of six to realize the assumed 3 percent annual growth in food production.

Three main factors explain the differences in the food import burden between these two groups of countries. First, the average energy content of the national food supply in 1978–80 was 83 percent of the FAO/WHO requirement in the six countries, and 91 percent in the thirty-one countries. Second, the average export earnings were $25.20 per capita in the six countries in 1978–80, and $63.10 in the thirty-one countries. Third, annual population growth is projected to be 2.9 percent through 1990 in the six countries and 2.3 percent in the thirty-one countries.

To reduce chronic food insecurity substantially in, say, ten years will take significant efforts to expand agricultural production and the incomes of low-income groups, emphasis on strategies to generate employment, more efficient use of resources, and improved government programs. It will also require substantially increased external support, both financial and technical, even to approach the agricultural growth rates assumed here, as well as an international commitment to provide large increases in international assistance for food imports—that is, to provide more food aid.

Transitory Food Insecurity

Transitory food insecurity is a temporary decline in food consumption below acceptable levels. For nations, food security is temporarily undermined by fluctuations in international food prices, food production, and export incomes. For households, such insecurity can also arise when their incomes deteriorate. The lack of data on short-term fluctuations in food consumption makes it necessary to assess transitory food insecurity by looking at fac-

Figure 2-4. Actual and Projected per Capita Cereal Imports for Two Groups of Countries, 1978–80 and 1990

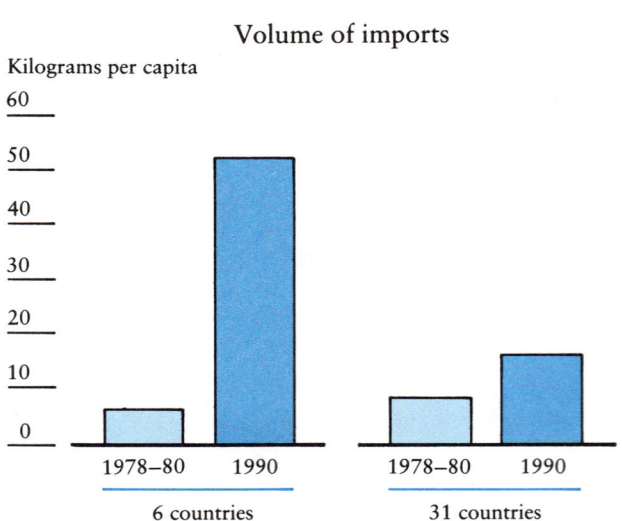

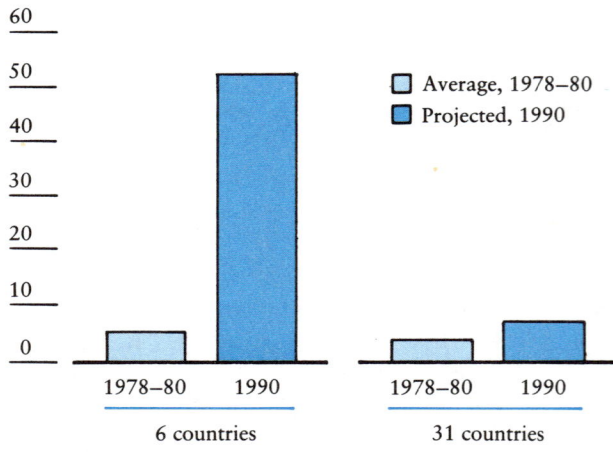

Six countries
Burkina Faso, Ethiopia, Mali, Nepal, Tanzania, Uganda

Thirty-one countries
Afghanistan, Bolivia, Botswana, Burundi, Central African Rep., Chad, Congo, Dominican Rep., Ecuador, El Salvador, Gambia, Ghana, Guatemala, Honduras, India, Jordan, Kenya, Malawi, Mauritania, Mozambique, Niger, Nigeria, Panama, Peru, Rwanda, Sierra Leone, Somalia, Togo, Zaire, Zambia, Zimbabwe

Note: Estimates for 1990 assume: an energy content in the per capita national diet of 100 percent of FAO/WHO requirements, currently projected growth rates in population and export earnings, and an annual growth rate in food production of 3 percent (cereal equivalents).
Source: World Bank estimates

tors that typically influence food consumption. The joint fluctuations in several of these factors determine the severity of transitory food insecurity. For instance, an increase in the price of imported food may be partially offset by a simultaneous increase in the price of a country's exports. Similarly, a decline in food production may be aggravated by a concurrent drop in yields of exported crops. World food prices, domestic food prices, and household incomes have the largest effects on transitory food insecurity.

World Food Markets

Instability in international prices poses a significant threat to the food security of developing countries. During 1968–78, a decade that included the very high prices that elicited so much concern in the early 1970s, the coefficients of price variation ranged from about 20 percent for maize to 30 percent for wheat and 35 percent for rice (Table 2-7). This sharp escalation in volatility of grain prices occurred in spite of slightly declining instability in global grain production.

Several supply and demand factors led to the widely fluctuating prices of 1968–78. On the supply side, after years of support programs that created large grain reserves, the largest exporters deliberately reduced stocks, which dramatically lowered the proportion of stocks to total consumption. When several years of poor harvests followed, world grain supplies fell. The increasing instability

Table 2-7. Variability of World Grain Prices and Production, 1958–78

Grain	Percentage coefficient of variation[a] 1958–68	1968–78
Price (constant dollars)		
Wheat[b]	13.7	28.9
Rice[c]	9.9	36.8
Maize[d]	8.2	18.7
Production (tons)		
Wheat	6.9	5.1
Rice	3.7	2.8
Maize	4.6	4.4
All grains	3.7	2.5

a. The coefficient of variation is defined as the standard deviation of $(x_t - \hat{x}_t)/\hat{x}_t$, where x_t are annual price or production observations and $\hat{x}_t$ are the respective trend values.
b. U.S. No. 1, Soft Red Winter; Atlantic port price.
c. Thai 5 percent broken; milled Bangkok price.
d. U.S. No. 2, Yellow; Gulf port price.
Sources: World Bank calculations based on USDA data; FAO, *FAO Production Yearbook,* various years.

in demand for imports reflected the sharp rise and subsequent fall in the growth of per capita income in developed and developing market economies, volatile exchange rates, the increasing pursuit of national policies that stabilized domestic prices irrespective of international price fluctuations, and new policies in centrally planned economies to use imports to offset sharp fluctuations in their food production.

The destabilizing influence of government interventions is probably greatest in the international rice market, which, when compared with that for wheat and maize, is small in relation to global production. The price of rice has been much more volatile than that of maize, partly because demand for foodgrains is much less elastic than that for feedgrains since the latter is related to the more elastic demand for livestock products (see Box 2-2).

International cereal prices are likely to remain highly volatile in the future, although probably not as volatile as in the 1970s. One reason for this continuing instability is that many countries will continue to stabilize domestic prices through policies that insulate them from international markets. Such policies destabilize international markets by reducing or eliminating the domestic adjustment to changing economic conditions and forcing the burden on the international economy. Another reason is the variability in the exchange rates of major trading countries. In addition, the United States may not continue to carry the lion's share of stocks of food supplies during this period of budgetary stringency.

Domestic Food Markets

Three main factors affect the stability of domestic food markets in a country: food production, the border prices in local currencies, and the capability to import food. The domestic production of major staple foods was generally more volatile than global production during 1968–78. On average, coefficients of production variation in eighteen developing countries were 18 percent for wheat, 14 percent for maize, and 8 percent for rice. Globally, the respective coefficients were 5, 4, and 3 percent. In most developing countries, trade did little to stabilize the domestic food supply. The stability of domestic supply was somewhat higher than that of domestic production alone in ten of eighteen selected countries for wheat and in seven of twelve countries for maize (Table 2-8). Surprisingly, in the

Table 2-8. Variability of Production, Net Imports, and Total Supply for Wheat and Maize in Selected Developing Countries, 1968–78

Region and country	Production	Net imports	Production plus net imports
Wheat			
Sub-Saharan Africa			
Nigeria	9.5	19.7	21.5
East Asia and Pacific			
Korea, Rep. of	20.2	16.7	18.7
South Asia			
Bangladesh	23.5	44.8	56.2
India	9.0	6.6	181.2
Pakistan	5.1	7.6	137.2
Middle East and North Africa			
Algeria	19.6	16.0	34.3
Egypt	8.6	13.7	24.3
Iran	7.2	8.5	354.4
Iraq	43.0	29.8	285.9
Morocco	19.1	18.7	51.3
Portugal	32.7	12.3	37.5
Tunisia	22.3	8.4	31.6
Turkey	11.6	12.3	311.7
Yemen Arab Rep.	27.5	12.6	29.3
Latin America and the Caribbean			
Brazil	28.9	18.2	23.6
Colombia	19.5	23.7	27.7
Mexico	16.4	14.2	299.1
Peru	5.9	15.2	18.3
Maize			
East Asia and Pacific			
Philippines	6.7	6.2	476.5
Latin America and the Caribbean			
Argentina	20.5	24.2	27.3
Bolivia	5.9	5.7	620.9
Brazil	9.3	5.8	110.5
Chile	21.2	20.1	261.4
Colombia	7.0	6.7	310.6
Costa Rica	13.5	11.3	287.6
El Salvador	16.2	20.1	258.4
Guatemala	4.5	5.6	265.4
Honduras	5.6	5.8	281.5
Panama	20.9	14.8	875.7
Uruguay	30.1	30.3	517.2

Sources: FAO *Production Yearbook* and FAO *Trade Yearbook*, various issues.

remaining countries, domestic supplies were less stable than domestic production. The high instability in food imports during 1968–78 shows that even modest stabilization of the domestic supply requires countries to cope with highly variable levels of imports (or exports).

In many countries, border prices, the second factor, have been less stable than domestic producer

Box 2-2. Can Grain Fed to Livestock Ease Transitory Food Insecurity?

Livestock consume a large share of grain in many countries. When there are shortfalls in grain production, herds can be reduced, which frees up more grain for direct human consumption. Such actions can significantly affect the total supply of food, since animals tend not to convert grain into food efficiently. It is more efficient to have people consume this grain directly.

The experience of the United States in 1974 illustrates how grain can be released for human consumption. There was a large shortfall in the maize crop that year. Reductions in livestock and poultry production, however, released almost 30 million tons of grain from the livestock sector between 1973 and 1975. As a result, the United States was able to sustain its maize exports at a time of strong international demand, and, thus, to sustain food supplies for other countries. Without this released grain, prices would have been much higher.

The question arises: to what extent can such responses provide a reserve that can be diverted to meet human needs? The answer is that it is a reserve, but a limited one. Not only is some feedgrain regarded as unsuitable for human consumption, but an increase in the price of feedgrain does not always reduce the demand. In addition, declines in demand tend to lag behind increases in the price of feedgrain.

About one-third of the world's grain production was fed to livestock in 1983 and 1984 and was distributed as shown in Box Figure 2-2. Coarse grains, mainly maize, make up more than 80 percent of the feedgrain. Only about 15 percent is wheat, and some of that has either sprouted or cannot be processed for human consumption. Rice is rarely used as feedgrain, but it is the major food source in Asia. Coarse grain is an important food source in some parts of the world, such as Africa and Mexico. Wheat is the food staple throughout Europe, North Africa, the Middle East, and the Soviet Union. Thus, adjustments in the livestock sector in industrial countries could help stabilize the prices of coarse grains, but not those of wheat and rice (though wheat and maize compete at the margin as a feedgrain).

Another problem is that feedgrain is not always released immediately by the livestock sector when its price increases. The profitability of feeding grain to livestock depends on both grain and livestock prices. When the ratio of livestock prices to grain

Box Figure 2-2. Global Distribution of Feedgrain, 1983–84
(percent)

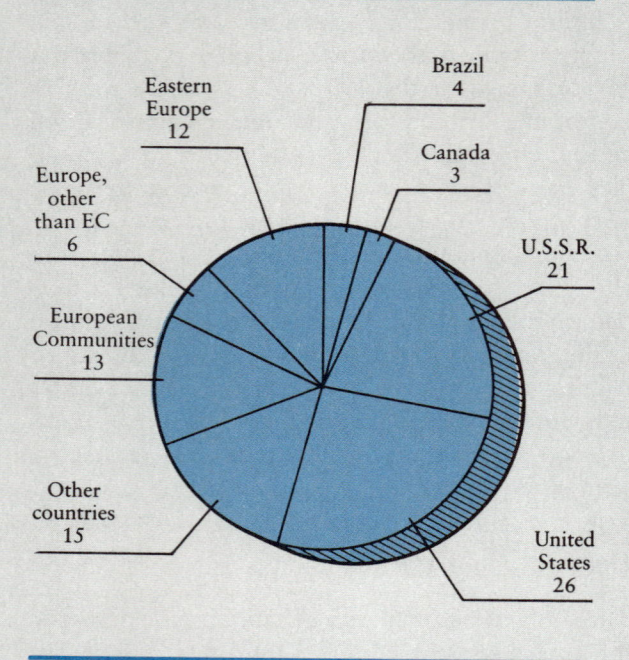

- Eastern Europe 12
- Brazil 4
- Canada 3
- Europe, other than EC 6
- U.S.S.R. 21
- European Communities 13
- United States 26
- Other countries 15

Note: Approximately 540 million tons of feedgrain were used.
Source: USDA (1984).

---

prices for some foods. The instability of wheat border prices is shown in Table 2-9. If governments had transmitted the instability of border prices to their domestic markets or had allowed domestic prices to vary in response to fluctuations in production, producers and consumers alike—particularly many poor people—would have felt significant shocks to their incomes and food budgets. Clearly, price-stabilizing trade policies and buffer stocks have kept domestic wheat prices more stable than they would have been under a completely free trading regime or without any trade. In many countries, however, actions to stabilize consumption and price when domestic production and the international price have been highly unstable have produced a very unstable wheat import bill.

prices is rising, livestock production becomes more profitable, and the use of grain as feed increases. When the ratio is low or declining, the demand for grain tends to shrink. Thus, if livestock prices rise, increases in grain prices can be tolerated. Other factors, such as changes in feeding efficiency and in the nonfeed costs of production, can also affect profitability.

Another factor at play is the way in which prices for several large livestock producers are insulated from the movements of the world market. In the U.S.S.R. which uses more than 100 million tons of feedgrain a year and is the second largest grain feeder and a major feed importer, use and importation of feed depend more on central planning decisions than on price ratios. Since the early 1970s, Soviet policy has been to stabilize meat consumption rather than slaughter more cattle and thus to destabilize meat supplies when feed supplies are scarce.

It usually is more profitable to invest less in feedgrain when the ratio of livestock prices to grain prices is low, whether through purchasing feed substitutes or reducing animal stocks. The need for immediately available feed substitutes can be a problem. Another way to reduce the consumption of feedgrain is to adjust animal stocks, something that cannot be done overnight on a large scale without draconian measures.

In summary, the extent to which the livestock sector can be a buffer for grain supplies depends on the availability and technical feasibility of grain substitutes, the extent to which feeding rates are adjusted, and the extent to which herd numbers can be adjusted. These depend in turn on the price incentives livestock producers receive and the speed at which they respond to them. As the U.S. experience with the 1974 grain shortfall shows, the response of maize use to the ratio of livestock prices to maize prices is not immediate, although it can be significant.

The capability to import food, the third factor influencing transitory food insecurity, has also been highly volatile. Developing countries are hard-pressed to stabilize domestic food prices if their foreign exchange earnings are unstable. Between 1968 and 1978, the average coefficient of variation of export earnings was 14 percent in twenty-seven low-income developing countries, 16 percent in fifty-two middle-income developing countries, and 9 percent in sixteen industrial market economies. The cost of nonfood imports probably was also more volatile in the developing than in the developed countries. In addition, developing countries seldom have the foreign exchange reserves to buffer fluctuations in current earnings. Prior commitments to such outlays as debt repayments and fuel imports restrict the use of foreign exchange for stabilization, and many countries have exhausted their borrowing possibilities when it becomes necessary to import additional food.

Few developing countries have been able to stabilize domestic food prices as much as industrial food-importing countries have. For instance, the average coefficient of variation for the domestic producer price of wheat from 1968 to 1978 in the eighteen developing countries shown in Table 2-9 was an estimated 12 percent, compared with about 5 percent in ten industrial countries. The greater variation for developing countries reflects higher

Table 2-9. Variability of Border Price, Producer Price, and Import Bill for Wheat in Selected Developing Countries, 1968–78

Region and country	Border price in local currency	Producer price	Import bill
Sub-Saharan Africa			
Nigeria	46.8	21.3	21.8
East Asia and Pacific			
Korea, Rep. of	39.7	12.1	31.5
South Asia			
Bangladesh	18.3	30.7	91.7
India	23.6	7.8	92.3
Pakistan	61.5	5.1	114.4
Middle East and North Africa			
Algeria	39.7	7.0	56.6
Egypt	37.4	7.0	57.3
Iran	35.8	11.4	84.1
Iraq	34.8	13.0	75.8
Morocco	34.1	9.1	65.4
Portugal	26.4	4.0	46.8
Tunisia	34.3	5.7	20.2
Turkey	37.5	18.1	300.0
Yemen Arab Rep.	27.5	8.6	38.5
Latin America and the Caribbean			
Brazil	36.2	18.2	38.5
Colombia	39.5	15.4	46.3
Mexico	28.1	8.3	148.8
Peru	28.2	10.7	33.8

Sources: Border prices imputed from FOB prices published in World Bank (1983). IMF exchange rate and World Bank transport data were used to calculate border prices. FAO (1982).

instability in the demand for food—because of highly unstable household incomes—and the uneven availability of foreign exchange. These countries also are less able to afford the budgetary drains and losses in resource efficiency from domestic programs that isolate their food and agricultural sectors from international markets.

Household Incomes

Because increases in production or incomes in one part of the country offset declines in another, aggregate data usually hide more than they reveal about how transitory food insecurity affects households. Data for India show that incomes, food prices, food consumption, and per capita cereal production were relatively stable in 1968, 1969, and 1970. But survey data of the per capita income and spending of about 4,000 rural households throughout India revealed high interyear variability. In nearly half of the households, income in any one year was more than 30 percent lower than their three-year average. A smaller sample of village households surveyed for four years in the late 1970s showed only slightly more stability. Although these data are likely to overstate the problem, they do show that the income and spending of rural households are highly unstable.

Data on Africa corroborate these findings. In northern Nigeria, the food consumption of 200 households in two villages fluctuated greatly between 1977 and 1978. In about a third of the households, consumption fell more than 30 percent; in about a sixth, consumption rose more than 30 percent. In 1978, a drought drove up the prices of staples produced and consumed locally. Only farmers with large marketable surpluses increased consumption that year.

Famines

Famines are the worst form of transitory food insecurity, for when food consumption plummets unexpectedly, widespread death and disease often follow (see Box 2-3). Famines can be caused by crop failures, natural and manmade calamities such

---

Box 2-3. How Rural Households Try to Cope with Transitory Food Insecurity

During a bad crop year, the regular seasonal adaptations of poorer households are thrown out of balance, and the poor are forced to dispose of their assets at bargain prices, usually to the rich. They have few things to sell and little or nothing to fall back on when successive bad harvests occur. In Sidamo province in the south of Ethiopia, three rainless years have made it difficult for cattleherders to sell their drought-starved animals. In the past, a bull would sell for about $200. During the drought a lean bull sold for $20 to $40 at most. To make things worse, grain prices increased while cattle prices dropped.

In such times of hardship, many poor families are forced to split up or gather food from the bush. Children are swapped between families in a village, sent to live with relatives in other areas, or even sold. When the harvest is bad, some family members migrate to leave more food for the rest of the family and to find work where the harvest has been better. Among the Bambara of Mali, the women often work in neighboring villages, where the harvest is better, in return for millet brought back to the household. In some cases, individuals find off-farm employment (in mining or even prostitution), and send income back to their families. When food is very scarce, whole families migrate, as frequently happens among fishing families on Ghana's coast during droughts.

For some households, "famine" foods gathered from the bush are vital for survival. Among the Bambara of Mali, poorer households supplement their diets with wild grasses and baobab seeds. In times of drought in The Gambia, women cultivate "hungry millet" (findi). Even if rainfall is very light, this type of millet can be grown because the crop matures in sixty days. Cropping trees to feed livestock during droughts is also common among African pastoralists. In extreme cases in India, Ethiopia, and Bangladesh, the starving eat a drought-resistant legume, known as kessari dal, even though it can lead to paralysis. Since poor families draw on these famine foods in times of need, more research is needed to identify all sources of such foods, to understand fully how they are used, to determine what can be done to ensure their availability during periods of stress, and to develop a nontoxic variety of kessari dal or a processing method that will eliminate the toxic effects.

as floods and wars, loss of real income or purchasing power, and other factors. Famines sometimes are caused by higher food prices, but not always.

As Sen's research (1981) on four particularly disastrous famines clearly shows, a decline in the general availability of food rarely causes a famine. Indeed, by paying excessive attention to changes in aggregate food supplies, governments and other organizations have sometimes not recognized the many other causes of famines.

Although the decline or collapse of food supplies may have played a primary role in some famines, the loss of real income better explains why famines occur and who gets hurt. A subsistence farmer whose harvest is lost or the wage worker whose source of employment disappears have both lost real income and therefore have lost purchasing power. Typically, victims belong to one or several groups:

- Small-scale farmers or tenants whose crops have failed and who cannot find other employment in agriculture (the Wollo in Ethiopia in 1973)
- Landless agricultural workers who lose their jobs when agricultural production declines (Bangladesh in 1974) or who face rapidly rising food prices and constant or declining wages (the Great Bengal famine of 1943)
- Other rural people, including destitutes and beggars, who are affected by a decline in real income in the famine regions (almost all famines)
- Pastoralists who get most of their food by selling animals for foodgrains; their herds may be ravaged by the drought, or animal prices may collapse relative to foodgrain prices (the Harerghe region of Ethiopia in 1974 and the drought-stricken Sahel in 1973).

War and other conditions interfering with food supplies seriously aggravate—but rarely cause—famines. Conversely, famine deaths can occur even when foodgrain markets are working very well. In several famines, local food prices barely rose, and food was continuously available, but the victims had no purchasing power. Famines can also occur during either economic booms or slumps. In Bengal in 1943, the increased demand for food fueled by gains in urban income inflated food prices faster than rural wages grew for the landless. In Ethiopia, however, a slump (caused partly by the 1974 drought) reduced effective food demand even as food supplies declined, so prices barely rose.

Whether local or widespread, famines inevitably are class-specific: the poor always suffer the most. Although sharp increases in the availability of food in the market can help prevent a famine, such an intervention is generally not enough. The social groups who suffer real losses of income must be provided with food, money, or employment. The following chapters examine the various options for doing this. The preliminary steps are to diagnose a famine early and to determine who needs help most and first. This diagnosis requires careful analysis —not just of the availability of food but of the potential effects of the famine on the real incomes and reserves of all social groups, especially the poor.

3

National Measures to Reduce Chronic Food Insecurity

Economic growth ultimately provides most households with the incomes to acquire enough food. Only the sick, elderly, unemployed, unemployable, or other disadvantaged groups then need transfer payments from relatives or the rest of society. But economic growth takes time. The search for remedies for chronic food insecurity must therefore go in two complementary directions. One is to explore ways to speed economic growth and to ensure the equitable distribution of its fruits; the other is to find more immediate ways to raise the ability of those facing chronic food insecurity to acquire food. This chapter considers mainly remedies of the second kind.

Some changes in policy will both promote efficient economic growth and raise the incomes of the poor—and hence improve their food security. In some cases, this might be achieved by shifting resources from large farms to small farms, from export crops to food crops, from industry to agriculture, or from capital-intensive to labor-intensive activities. If so, such shifts should be encouraged as part of an effective policy for food security. Similarly, raising prices of agricultural commodities to border prices (at a realistic exchange rate) is good for growth and food security if those facing chronic food insecurity are mostly farmers producing a marketable surplus.

The scope for policy change of this kind is probably widest in the lowest-income countries and wherever a high proportion of the chronically food insecure has access to land. Policies that promote efficiency in agriculture are also likely to improve the incomes of many of the poor in these countries.

But policies that speed economic growth will not be enough to achieve adequate food security for all groups in a reasonable time. That will require more direct measures that may involve tradeoffs between growth and the achievement of food security in the short and medium run. Increasing food security is an objective of most governments because of its humanitarian, political (that is, strategic), and economic importance; it is of particular concern in a period of policy adjustments. Measures to enhance food security or to reduce the adverse effect of other policy changes can make the needed adjustment policies more acceptable. Each country will have to decide how best to minimize these tradeoffs.

Overview of Policy Interventions

Three major interventions can be used to improve food security. The first influences the food supply through changes in domestic production, imports (including food aid), or exports. Such changes may or may not affect the domestic price of food. If they do, the effect is marketwide and affects all consumers and producers of that food. The second intervention reduces prices of specific foods sold to some or all consumers without altering the prices paid to producers. Government funds offset the gap between the price paid by consumers and the price received by producers. The third intervention augments incomes by means other than changing food prices, such as by subsidizing employment, subsidizing nonfood commodities, or providing transfers of income in cash or kind. The second and third interventions can be targeted or marketwide. Countries with access to food aid can use it to support the implementation of any of these interventions.

Whether or not they are supported by food aid, these three policy interventions are likely to have different short-run effects on the three main groups of people facing chronic food insecurity: the urban poor, the rural landless, and the small-scale farmers (Table 3-1). Interventions that increase incomes or reduce consumer prices without lowering producer prices clearly improve food security. With such interventions, none of the people facing chronic food insecurity would suffer a decline in their real income. In contrast, there are food supply policies that may increase food security for some poverty groups but reduce it for others. In addition, some of the initial effects of interventions can be eroded over time. For instance, lower food prices may eventually lead to lower nominal wages. The long-run gains to workers would then be limited largely to the growth in employment from the implicit wage subsidy. Since all interventions have costs, a comprehensive analysis of the size and incidence of benefits would have to take into account the direct and indirect effects (such as changes other than those in food prices and employment) of these costs.

Targeted Interventions

Ideally, a targeted intervention increases the real income and food consumption of a target population without the cost of bringing those benefits to the rest of the population. Distributing rationed food at concessionary prices to a specified group, without affecting the open market price of food, is one targeted intervention. Another is to give small farmers rationed inputs (say, fertilizers) at less than full cost or to give them an opportunity to sell some of their produce at above-market prices. In practice, it is rarely possible to design programs that benefit the target population exclusively.

Targeted interventions have several common features. First, they usually achieve food security without significantly interfering with other goals, such as the efficient allocation of resources. Second, they demand considerably more managerial capability to identify and reach the right people than do marketwide interventions. Third, their fiscal costs are also high compared with the often low budgetary requirements of price-reducing trade interventions—something to be carefully considered when budget deficits are running high, as they now are in many countries.

Table 3-1. Direct Effects of Interventions on Chronic Food Insecurity

| | | \multicolumn{6}{c}{Effect on chronic food insecurity} |
Kind of intervention	Price of food	Urban poor Nominal income	Urban poor Real income	Rural landless Nominal income	Rural landless Real income	Small-scale farmers Nominal income	Small-scale farmers Real income
Increasing the food supply							
Trade							
Reducing imports	+	0	−	(+)	(−)	+	+
Expanding imports	−	0	+	(−)	(+)	−	−
Subsidizing food production							
Traded foods	0	0	0	(+)	(+)	(+)	+
Nontraded foods	−	0	+	(+)	+	(+)	(+)
Subsidizing food prices for consumers (while maintaining producer prices)							
Targeted or marketwide	−	0	+	0	+	0	+
Augmenting incomes							
Targeted or marketwide	0	+	+	+	+	+	+

Note: 0 = no effect; + = improvement; − = deterioration. Parentheses indicate a slight effect.
Source: World Bank data.

Governments also have to cope with pressure from private interest groups that want to divert program funds from the target groups. In fact, many programs become vehicles to enhance the power of government bureaucracies. This often creates a political paradox in which there is greatest support for ineffective programs and least for effective ones.

Another concern is the disincentive effects of targeted interventions on the supply of labor. It is feared that the recipients will have their consumption needs met without having to provide labor and that they may become completely dependent on government support. If the targeted group is really at the margin of subsistence, however, improving their nutrition is likely to enhance their physical ability and motivation to perform useful work. Clearly, if the targeting is restricted to the truly needy and the extent of the consumption subsidy is limited to boosting them above the margin of subsistence, any disincentive effects will be negligible and probably more than offset by the effect of improved well-being on their capacity and desire to work. The importance of the disincentive effect thus depends on the nature of the intervention.

Marketwide Interventions

Unlike targeted interventions, marketwide interventions change the open-market prices all people pay or receive for consumer goods and farm inputs. For example, restricting food imports lowers the real income of those who purchase food, but it increases the income of those who sell domestically produced food. The sale of inputs to all farmers at a subsidized price is also a marketwide intervention that will increase the real income of those who use the subsidized inputs, but in an open economy, in which food is freely traded, it may have no effect on the prices consumers pay for food.

The most attractive feature of marketwide policies is that they are quickly and easily implemented. For instance, if a government wants to increase the incomes of farmers who produce a commodity that is also imported, it can simply impose an import duty. If, similarly, the government wants to increase the incomes of farmers who produce a commodity for export, it can create an export subsidy. In the same way, an import subsidy can be easily instituted to increase the supply of a food.

Some marketwide policies can be implemented without placing great demands on the government budget. For instance, the price of a domestically produced food can be lowered by allowing imports to increase. If imports are available to the government as food aid, they can be sold to provide a source of added revenue. If food is exported (as rice is in Thailand), its price in the domestic market can be reduced by imposing an export tax. This also gives the government added revenue. Because marketwide interventions often convey benefits to a large segment of the population, they tend to be more popular and thus more politically sustainable than programs exclusively for the poor.

Many marketwide policies raise the real income of some groups that face chronic food insecurity at the expense of others, however, especially if food prices are held down. If the group adversely affected by the intervention is small, it can be compensated by other interventions. But if the livelihood of, say, half of those facing chronic food insecurity depends on the sale of food, any intervention to keep food prices low may make the remedy worse than the problem. The same is true if high food prices for farmers cause the real income of a large proportion of the landless or urban poor to drop.

Many marketwide policies intended to lower consumer prices also lower producer prices. When this happens, it is important to assess the efficiency losses: the cost of diverting resources to the production of lower-value commodities. In making the choice between an income transfer program to a target group and a trade intervention that distorts the price of food to producers, it is necessary to compare the cost of administering the first with the efficiency losses of the second in relation to how each increases food security.

Increasing the Food Supply

There are two kinds of food supply intervention: some try to change the volume of food exports or imports, while others seek to increase domestic production, say, by subsidizing inputs or investing in agricultural infrastructure. Two fundamental questions need to be asked about how a supply intervention will affect chronic food insecurity. Does it affect the availability and price of food and hence the real income of people facing chronic food insecurity? Does it increase their nominal earnings?

Interventions that affect the volume of food trade always change the availability and price of food, which in turn affect consumption, domestic production, and food self-sufficiency. When food is internationally traded, interventions to increase domestic production generally do not add to the availability of food and thus do not change the price of food. Instead, they tend to expand exports or substitute for food imports and thus change only the level of self-sufficiency (see Box 3-1). When food is not traded, however, these interventions increase the availability of food and reduce its price.

Trade Interventions

Most developing countries have pursued a variety of trade, aid, and exchange rate policies that have kept domestic food prices lower than border prices (under a realistic exchange rate). These policies have recently come under attack, mainly because they have led to underinvestment in food production. In the long run, this underinvestment, like that in other sectors with high potential, inhibits economic growth, the reduction of poverty, and the achievement of food security.

The short-run effect of lower food prices on food security is not clear-cut, however. In countries in which many of the people facing chronic food insecurity are rural landless or urban poor who must buy their food, lower food prices will improve food security. In countries in which many of the poor produce more food than they consume, however, lower food prices will worsen food security. And in countries in which many of the poor are subsistence farmers who neither sell nor buy food, food prices have no effect on food security. Thus, it should not be presumed that only the urban poor benefit from lower food prices and that the rural poor are always better off with higher prices. In fact, there is considerable evidence to the contrary.

An analysis of the energy content of per capita food consumption, income, and food prices in twenty-nine countries in 1975 showed that food security, measured by the energy content of the national diet, increases as the price of food decreases when income is held constant (see Annex C). Another study (Binswanger and Quizon 1984) showed the effects of alternative trade policies on chronic food insecurity in an agricultural sector model of India. A simulated increase of wheat

---

Box 3-1. Is Self-Sufficiency Essential for Food Security?

National self-sufficiency in tradable foods is efficient only when a country has a comparative advantage in producing those foods. Moreover, food security is achieved only if all households have the ability to buy this food. Thus, there is no necessary link between self-sufficiency and food security.

Two empirical studies corroborate this conclusion. One is a statistical analysis of food security over time for fifty developing countries (see Annex C). The study shows a strong association between the energy content of the national diet, which is used as a proxy for chronic food insecurity, and per capita income. It also shows that variations in self-sufficiency in cereal supply explain little or none of the variation in the energy content of the national diet. Although the results need to be interpreted cautiously, they provide some confirmation that self-sufficiency has no intrinsic value for eliminating chronic food insecurity.

The other study (Binswanger and Quizon 1984) shows that an increase in domestic food production in India will not reduce food insecurity unless it reduces food prices. These results are consistent with the findings that per capita food consumption in India has remained fairly constant for many years despite growth in per capita production. Even high food production does little to enhance food security if the additional food produced substitutes for imports or is exported.

Development and technological progress of agriculture are, of course, important sources of economic growth. India, for example, could not have prevented an increase of chronic food insecurity without taking advantage of agricultural technology and other productive investments to boost agricultural production. Food grain production in India rose from 90 million tons in 1970 to 130 million tons by 1985. The value of this additional food, if it had had to be imported, would have been on the order of 10 billion dollars. It is difficult to imagine developments in any other sector that could have contributed as much to food security as those which led to this rapid expansion of food production.

imports equal to 10 percent of the existing supply in the 1970s would have led to price declines in domestic foods: the wheat price would decline 15 percent, the rice price 6 percent, and the coarse cereal price 5 percent. There would have been a 5 percent drop in wheat production and a slight increase in rice and coarse cereal production. As a result, real income and cereal consumption for the lowest quartile in the urban population would have risen about 5 percent. For the lowest quartile of the rural population, the net effect on the real income and cereal consumption would also have been positive, although much less so. Significantly, the lower food prices more than compensated the poorest rural group for the drop in employment and wages. The second quartile in the rural population would neither gain nor lose. Thus, at least in India, trade interventions resulting in lower food prices would reduce chronic food insecurity for the most vulnerable segments of both the rural and the urban poor (see Box 3-2).

The cost-effectiveness of any trade interventions to improve food security will depend on the leakages to unintended beneficiaries, the income losses of the poor who are adversely affected by the price change, and the losses in efficiency from price distortions in production. The tradeoffs need to be examined in each case. For example, maintaining an overvalued exchange rate will cause resources to be misallocated throughout the economy, with all tradable goods underpriced relative to nontradable goods. Although an overvalued exchange rate may thus slow economic growth because of inefficient use of resources, it can hold food prices down if food products are tradable goods. A drastic devaluation in the interests of efficiency can cause food prices to rise and thus harm many of the urban poor and rural landless. The prospect of a devaluation is good reason to consider compensatory measures. Targeted programs can be cost-effective and thus are one alternative. If such programs are not feasible, food imports might be temporarily subsidized to soften the effects of a devaluation on the food security of the poor.

Trade interventions to reduce the price of a specific food will be more cost-effective the more the food is consumed by people who face chronic food insecurity and is produced by farmers who do not. Another key consideration is the price responsiveness of domestic output of different foods: the less responsive the price is, the less efficiency will be lost from the price intervention. The reverse is also true, of course.

In many countries producer prices for agricultural commodities have been kept below border prices, with serious consequences for the agricultural sector and the incomes of rural people. Efforts to accelerate growth and raise agricultural productivity generally include increasing producer prices or freeing them from controls. If, however, much of the marketed surplus of domestically supplied food is not produced by the chronically food insecure but many of the net purchasers of food are chronically food insecure, their food security can decrease, at least temporarily, when food prices are raised. Interventions to enhance food security thus require a balanced, empirical analysis of the effects of changing food prices in each country.

Production Subsidies

Developing countries have often been criticized—and rightly—for investing too little in agriculture and discriminating against food production. At issue here, however, is whether unsatisfactory food production—even more than unsatisfactory economic development—is at the root of chronic food insecurity (Pinstrup-Andersen 1983; Reutlinger 1983b). Should special subsidies be used to promote food production? If so, when? Special encouragement to producers of food crops may improve food security either by raising the incomes of producers or by lowering food prices to consumers. It is important to distinguish here between tradable and nontradable foods.

For tradable foods, measures to support production will increase the income of producers. To increase food security, the tradable crops supported should be grown mainly by small-scale farmers or should provide a major source of employment for the rural poor. An example of the latter is vegetable production in Mexico. But the food security of consumers cannot be improved by subsidizing the production of tradable foods, since this will not lower food prices. For nontradable foods, since production support measures will reduce consumer prices, food security will improve if crops consumed by the poor, rather than those produced by the poor, are supported. For instance, subsidizing the production of locally consumed foods in isolated regions of a country may be the most cost-effective way to raise the real income of

Box 3-2. Food Policy Interventions in India

Most of this report discusses the costs and effects of interventions in an essentially open economy (and in the context of a partial equilibrium). But some large and poor economies, such as Bangladesh, China, and India, are not open. The state controls trade in food and many nonfood items. Food imports and food aid therefore have substantial price effects on all agricultural goods—effects that will later alter agricultural supplies and the demand for labor. Technological change can have a much greater effect on prices in a closed economy than in an open one. In the long run such changes in the price of food will affect labor supply decisions and hence wages—the most important source of income for the poor.

A general equilibrium model of the Indian agricultural sector developed at the World Bank captures many of the direct and indirect effects of changes in the supply of a particular food and of income transfer payments. The model determines the production, prices, and consumption of rice, wheat, and coarse cereals and analyzes the consequences of policies for agricultural wages, employment, and profits. It then computes the real income of four rural and four urban quartiles of per capita spending. All calculations are based on 1973 values. Three questions concerning food policy are examined: first, to whom should the subsidy be targeted; second, should increases in food demand be accommodated by extra imports; and third, how should the subsidy be financed? Five results emerge from simulations using this model.

First, price increases substantially erode any income transfer to the poor—say, through "fair-price" shops—unless the added food demand of the poor is accommodated by added imports (or reduced exports). Suppose, for example, that $350 million worth of rice and wheat, or 1.25 million metric tons of wheat and 0.5 million tons of rice, is distributed through "fair-price" shops to all urban groups. If these extra food grains are imported, the real income of the urban poor increases 7.5 percent. If the extra food grains are not imported, higher food prices will erode these benefits to 2.8 percent.

Second, added imports benefit all net buyers of food. The release of $350 million worth of aid-financed wheat (10 percent of India's wheat supply in 1973) depresses wheat prices by 19 percent and wheat production by about 6 percent. The prices of rice and coarse cereals decline less, but their output increases as resources are shifted to them from wheat. Aggregate agricultural output thus declines only 0.2 percent. The main beneficiaries of this policy are the urban groups, particularly the poorest, whose real income rises 6 percent. The poorest rural quartile, mainly landless workers, experiences a gain of 1.7 percent; the second quartile, mostly subsistence farmers, neither gains nor loses. Aggregate farm profits decline, and the richer half of the rural population bears this loss.

Third, the estimated long-run gain by the rural poor from the extra wheat imports is substantially less than the short-run gain. (These much larger short-run gains have been estimated in a general equilibrium study by de Janvry and Subbarao [1984].) Two mechanisms erode the short-run gains of the rural poor. First, the demand for labor is reduced slightly as agricultural production declines. More important, the declining food prices increase the real rural wage and the labor supply. Only a drop in the nominal wage can bring the labor market back to balance. This implies that more substantial and lasting income transfers can be made to the rural landless only through targeted food subsidies or employment programs.

Fourth, the method used to finance food procurement can either reinforce or offset the income transfers of food policy in subtle ways. For example, taxing the rural rich through a forced procurement scheme reduces aggregate food demand (and food prices) more than does an equivalent excise tax on all nonagricultural commodities.

Fifth, the poor benefit more from agricultural development than from development in other sectors of the economy only if food prices decline. A simulation shows that the early gains of the Green Revolution were almost exclusively from added farm profits. Real farm profits increased almost 50 percent from 1965–66 to 1970–71. Net sellers of food captured most of the benefits because the gains in production were used mainly to reduce imports, and domestic terms of trade moved in favor of agriculture. Once self-sufficiency had been nearly reached, further production gains reversed the movement of the terms of trade. Between 1970–71 and 1975–76 real farm profits declined about 15 percent, and the gains from increased productivity were transferred from net sellers of food to net buyers.

the poor in those areas.

Everything said about food production also applies to food processing and marketing. Because the goal is to reduce the cost of food to consumers, the price that matters is the retail price (wholesale cost plus the marketing margin). Efficient marketing is important for economic welfare, but subsidizing the marketing of food is justified only if this is the most cost-effective way to raise the real income of those facing chronic food insecurity.

Subsidizing Food Prices

Reducing the prices food producers receive has at least two negative consequences. First, low food prices inhibit incentives, compromise resource efficiency, and reduce growth—thus indirectly inhibiting food security. Second, they can depress the real income of low-income households that are net sellers of food—thus directly inhibiting food security. Reducing food prices for consumers (without depressing producer prices) has fewer adverse consequences if the interventions are cost-effective. In considering such subsidized prices, it is important to distinguish between targeted and marketwide subsidies.

Targeted Subsidies

The most popular targeted intervention is the food ration program, which distributes food at a concessionary price to selected groups of households. In many cases rations are not restricted to the neediest, either because of administrative difficulties in identifying them or because the program serves several political purposes. Because it is difficult to manage distribution in sparsely settled or inaccessible areas, ration programs for the rural poor are rare. The experience of India's fair price shops is a prime example of the difficulties of restricting access to rations in urban areas and of reaching the rural poor.

Problems can arise even when food ration programs are successfully targeted. One problem is inflexibility in the way a program determines who is eligible, as exemplified by Sri Lanka's food stamp program. The target group was identified by household size and earnings, but, because households were never checked to see if they remained eligible, many stayed on the rolls even after their earnings increased above the eligibility cutoff. Households that became eligible after the program started, however, never had a chance to get on the rolls. Another problem is that some food may leak into the open market. But if people know their entitlement and if violations are policed, food rations to small groups can be far more cost-effective than marketwide subsidies.

If a high density of people is facing chronic food insecurity in isolated areas, unrationed food can be distributed at a slightly subsidized price through publicly controlled stores. But the difference between the subsidized price and the open market price must not be so large that it becomes profitable to resell the food in the open market. An example of a successful unrationed food subsidy is the Rede Somar program in Northeast Brazil. When the government realized that the cost of staple foods in small retail outlets in poor neighborhoods was 20 to 30 percent higher than in supermarkets elsewhere, it began to supply food in these neighborhoods at a price that was the same as, or slightly lower than, prices in the supermarkets. The cost of the program has been small because food prices were reduced without incurring the high costs of distributing food rations.

Food can sometimes be distributed efficiently at a concessional price in conjunction with other programs, such as feeding at schools or distributing food coupons at health centers. The eligible can be identified by clear criteria, such as living near the school or clinics or having diagnosable symptoms of malnutrition. In such programs the added administrative cost of distributing the food rations or coupons can be low.

In assisting projects like these over the years, the World Bank has learned that some form of targeting is usually feasible and that targeting does indeed lower food costs and improve the nutrition of the target groups. Food subsidy programs in Brazil and Columbia, as well as feeding programs in Brazil, Indonesia, and India, use many approaches to identify the most vulnerable groups, such as the poorest households, pregnant and lactating women, or children under five years old whose growth is faltering. (see Box 3-3). This new emphasis on targeting is an important break from the past when mass coverage was the norm.

Marketwide Subsidies

One way to overcome the difficulties of targeting is to reduce prices of selected foods to all consumers without reducing the price paid to produc-

> **Box 3-3. Food Subsidy Programs in Brazil, Colombia, and India Assisted by the World Bank**
>
> Food assistance programs in Brazil, Colombia, and India have promoted the concept of selective participation. A coupon program that distributed food every two weeks through government-run supermarkets used income to determine who could participate in Recife, Brazil. The program revealed several problems.
>
> - It is difficult to target income if income reporting is arbitrary.
> - Food coupons are more effective at reducing child malnutrition if the subsidies are high enough to sustain participation.
> - A coupon program requires extensive bookkeeping and administrative cost.
> - Down payments for coupons pose a barrier to the lowest income group.
> - The system must adapt to the frequent small purchases that low-income families have to make.
>
> Building on lessons from the evaluations, the Brazilian program was modified, with apparent success, to reach very low-income neighborhoods without coupons or down payments. Common basic foods now are subsidized for all customers of many registered small neighborhood stores in selected poverty areas. Any leakage of benefits to people not in need is much less expensive than administering the cumbersome coupon program. The revised system also makes it possible for low-income families to make frequent small purchases.
>
> In Colombia areas of poverty were identified as part of the national development plan. Targets of food subsidies were then narrowed to households with children under five years old or a pregnant or lactating woman. This reduced the number of possible beneficiaries and thus lowered administrative and fiscal costs. Little leakage or fraudulent coupon use was apparent.
>
> In a feeding program in India's Tamil Nadu state the criterion for targeting was the growth of children. Children were admitted to the program when their growth faltered and were removed when their weight increased satisfactorily. Because of this selectivity the food cost was well below that of most feeding programs for preschool children. Mothers did not use the supplements as an excuse to reduce their children's intake at home because of a sense of shame if the child did not gain weight. (The same sort of shame, along with inconvenience, keeps the affluent from buying at subsidized shops in poor neighborhoods.) The project covered 9,600 villages—about a third of the state—and has averted an estimated 107,000 cases of severe malnutrition and 12,000 deaths. In addition, children who have been through the program are 1.75 kilograms heavier at age five than children from control villages.

ers. The government then finances the difference between the two prices. Marketwide subsidies are clearly more costly than targeted subsidies, but the administrative costs can be much lower and the coverage of the target population much broader.

Marketwide consumer subsidies do have difficulties. They generally require heavy government involvement in the wholesale food trade. The government must manage a two-price scheme—a higher price for producers and a lower price for consumers—and it must be possible to distinguish the food sold to consumers from the food bought from farmers. This is easy when the food is normally processed before it is consumed. For instance, the government can buy all marketed whole wheat at the border price and sell flour at a lower price. But the government must ensure that the selling price is not so low that it is profitable to use the food for other purposes, such as feeding livestock or making alcohol.

The main determinant of a food's suitability for subsidy is the share of it that goes to the target population. If a food is consumed exclusively by the target group, the subsidy will be very efficient; a dollar's worth of subsidy will provide almost a dollar of added income to the target group. But if the target population consumes only 30 percent of a subsidized food, the subsidy is much less efficient. This efficiency varies according to the food chosen. In Brazil, for example, a dollar spent on subsidizing bread transfers about 18 cents to the low-income population and a dollar spent on subsidizing legumes, about 39 cents (see Table 3-2 and Annex A). Food subsidies for consumers can be even more efficient if further selectivity is introduced by, say, subsidizing inferior grades consumed by the poor.

If most of the poor are net buyers of food, lowering food prices can redistribute income. Even poorly targeted food subsidies tend to benefit the poor more than the rich because they increase the incomes of the poor by a higher percentage. In

> **Box 3-4. Distribution of Food and Income in Egypt**
>
> Egypt has long had some form of government-supported food security program. Government involvement in consumer-oriented food policies has increased rapidly since the early 1970s when food subsidies amounted to about 1 percent of the budget. After 1974 these programs made up an average of 21 percent of current public spending and almost 7 percent of GDP. This high budgetary cost has led to enormous controversy—and to much research on its ramifications for the economy and the distribution of income, especially at the International Food Policy Research Institute (IFPRI) (Alderman and von Braun 1984; Scobie 1983).
>
> Nearly every Egyptian holds ration cards in a program that goes far beyond providing low-priced staple foods to the poor. Quotas of bread, flour, sugar, oil, tea, and rice, as well as seasonal quotas of beans and lentils, are available at subsidized prices. A second set of quotas, at higher but still subsidized prices, apply to sugar, oil, rice, and tea. Other commodities, such as frozen meat, can be bought through government cooperatives at higher prices, which still are lower than in the open market. In addition to the flour distributed through government channels and bakeries, a third to a half of the flour on the open market is imported and priced with an implicit subsidy.
>
> Most developing countries, by design or default, target food subsidies to the urban population. In Egypt, however, the benefits to the urban and rural poor are almost equally distributed when income transfers from strictly government channels are measured. When the effects of government-induced price distortions in the open market are also included, the chief beneficiaries of income transfers appear to be the rural population (see Box Table 3-4). This is partly because of the high protection on livestock products, of which the rural poor are the main producers. When urban consumers make their purchases on the open market, they lose because of the distortions.
>
> Despite the substantial bias of the subsidies toward the poor, certain aspects of the system favor upper-income groups. Some commodities are not available in sufficient amounts to meet demand at the official price, so people either have to wait longer in line at government outlets or have to buy their food on the open market. Since the rich can afford to make larger purchases at the cooperatives, they have more to gain by waiting than the poor. In addition, subsidies on frozen meat do not benefit the poor who do not buy it. (These subsidies were rescinded in 1984 to reduce the subsidy budget.)
>
> The parts of Egypt's complex system that favor the rich need to be further evaluated and the options for redistributing the benefits examined. With wheat taking nearly half the cost of food subsidies, however, the high budgetary outlays cannot be reduced much without greatly reducing the real cost of the wheat subsidy.
>
> The increase in subsidies has been financed through added loans, grants, and foreign exchange, but a large part has been covered by inflationary financing of the government deficit. One of IFPRI's studies (Scobie 1984) finds that a 10 percent rise in spending on subsidies has increased the inflation rate more than 5 percent, reduced international assets 2 percent, and devalued the free market exchange rate

Brazil a subsidy for rice transfers more income to the rich, and a subsidy for legumes transfers more to the poor. But the rice subsidy still redistributes income progressively; it produces a 1.6 percent change in per capita income for low-income groups and only a 0.2 percent change for high-income groups (Table 3-3).

Can developing countries afford to subsidize food prices on the scale needed to reduce chronic food insecurity? Rough calculations show that reducing prices of major staples in the diets of the poor by 20 percent will increase their average real income by about 5 to 10 percent. (This assumes that the poor spend 25 to 50 percent of their income on staple foods.) The poorest of the poor would undoubtedly realize an even larger increase in their purchasing power. Clearly, food price subsidies of this size can help in the short run. But what would be the cost? Cereal spending makes up about 15 percent of GDP in low-income countries and 8 percent in middle-income countries (Kravis 1982). Therefore, a 20 percent subsidy on cereals amounts to 3 and 1.6 percent, respectively, of the GDP of those countries. The budgetary costs can thus be considerable. Moreover, interests in such interventions become vested, making it politically difficult to eliminate them and in some cases causing them to burgeon out of control.

more than 3 percent.

The demand for imported food has become inelastic under the subsidy scheme. Because the industrial sector depends heavily on imported raw materials for current output and on imported capital goods for expansion, the subsidy scheme has important ramifications for this sector. If the price of imported food rises or the supply of foreign exchange falls, industrial imports are reduced to maintain food imports. The IFPRI study estimates that a 10 percent rise in the cost of imported food would result in a fall of 1 to 2 percent in industrial output, as imports of raw materials are crowded out to provide more foreign exchange for food imports. A fall in foreign exchange supplies of 10 percent would reduce industrial output 4 percent and investment 6 percent.

Egypt now faces difficult policy questions. The system of food subsidies is increasing the food security of the poor. The issue, however, is whether this can be done more cost-effectively by increased targeting of the subsidies. Two options are to distribute subsidized rations only to the poor and to subsidize only the foods that the poor spend a high share of their income on.

Box Table 3-4. Income Transfer Effects from the Food Subsidy and Pricing Policies
(percentage of annual per capita spending)

	Urban					Rural				
	Expenditure quartile[a]				All	Expenditure quartile[a]				All
Source of transfer	1st	2nd	3rd	4th	households	1st	2nd	3rd	4th	households
Government channels[b]	15.5	9.7	6.4	3.2	6.0	16.9	10.3	6.6	4.2	7.0
Open market (consumer)	−2.8	−3.3	−3.1	−3.4	−3.2	1.1	1.6	1.1	0.3	0.8
Total net consumer transfer	12.7	6.4	3.3	−0.2	2.8	18.0	11.9	7.7	4.5	7.8
Producer prices	0	0	0	0	0	−0.8	−0.5	−0.7	−1.2	−1.1
Total transfer[c]	12.7	6.4	3.3	−0.2	2.8	17.2	11.4	6.4	3.3	6.7

Note: Because of the difficulties inherent in assessing income, total expenditure has been used as a proxy for income. The income transfer is indicated by the percentage increase or decrease in per capita expenditure over or under the expenditures that would result if all food purchases were made at their international price equivalents.
a. The first expenditure quartile is the lowest income group; the fourth, the highest.
b. Includes ration shops, bakeries, and cooperatives.
c. Includes effects of distorted producer prices.
Source: Calculations from Alderman and von Braun (1984), table 20, based on 1982 household survey data from IFPRI and the Institute of National Planning, Cairo.

Whether such large transfer payments are affordable is an economic and financial issue as well as a matter of humanitarian and political judgment. There is also the further question of whether food subsidies simply reallocate current consumption or whether they also affect long-run growth. The answer depends on the tradeoff between reduced national and private savings and improved human capital formation (see Box 3-4).

Augmenting Incomes

Almost all governments have policies or programs to augment directly the incomes of disadvantaged groups, particularly the rural poor who cannot be reached by food price subsidies. Some interventions, such as unemployment insurance and public works programs, are clearly targeted to benefit specific groups. Other interventions, such as regional development schemes or subsidized inputs and credit, are less well targeted in that a share (sometimes a large share) of the benefits goes to people whose incomes are well above the poverty threshold. To the extent that the interventions do increase the income of the poor, they will improve their food security. But the net benefits may be small if the cost of the interventions is borne by

Table 3-2. Efficiency of a Price Subsidy on Selected Foods in Brazil and the Philippines

Food	Per capita consumption (grams per day) Target population[a]	Per capita consumption (grams per day) Total population	Approximate income transferred to target group per dollar of subsidy (cents)
Brazil			
Bread	30	58	18
Cassava	279	139	60
Legumes	88	68	39
Maize	35	26	40
Rice	86	111	23
Philippines			
Beef	8	17	16
Rice	274	285	37
Sugar	26	34	27
Wheat	29	44	23

a. The target population is assumed to be 30 percent of the total population.
Source: Williamson Gray (1982).

the poor through fewer investments in agriculture and fewer social services.

Targeted Interventions

The three main targeted interventions that governments use to augment incomes are public works programs, income transfers to the self-employed, and cash transfer payments.

In South Asia, there are already several public works programs aimed at improving food security. The main advantage of transferring income through employment rather than through transfer payments is that the programs can be self-targeting. Payment for employment, either in money or in kind, selectively conveys income to the poor during seasons in which they have few employment alternatives. Targeting is effective, however, only if wages for public employment are substantially below market wages. Otherwise, public employment will attract people other than the poor and will displace private employment.

The cost-effectiveness of public employment depends on the cost of the subsidy and the net income conveyed to the target group. The cost of the subsidy is the difference between the cost of the scheme and the value of the assets or public services that it generates. The net income conveyed is the difference between the wages paid and the costs to the participants. These costs include what they spend for travel to and from work, the extra cost of living away from home, and the income forgone from private employment, such as reduced food production at home or the cost of store-bought food for what would have been processed at home (see Box 3-5). A problem with public works programs is that they usually demand large fiscal expenditures. Even in a cost-effective program, the fiscal cost may be high because the assets or services produced are public goods that do not generate revenue for the government. Thus, the subsidy for public employment may mean low social costs but high financial outlays from the government.

It can be more cost-effective for a government to augment the incomes of some of the rural poor through explicit subsidies or transfers to the self-employed. These subsidies have the advantage of allowing people to remain where they are and to continue to put their land to productive use. They include distributing rationed inputs, procuring products by ration, and providing public services such as roads, education, and extension services in poverty regions. For example, if poor farming households use fertilizer, one way to augment their

Table 3-3. How Subsidies on Different Foods Affect Consumers at Different Income Levels in Brazil

Income group	Per capita income without subsidy (cruzeiros)	Per capita value of subsidy (cruzeiros) Rice	Per capita value of subsidy (cruzeiros) Legumes	Change in per capita income from subsidy (percent) Rice	Change in per capita income from subsidy (percent) Legumes
Low	1,347	21	34	1.6	2.5
Medium	3,237	30	25	1.0	0.8
High	15,609	27	18	0.2	0.1

Note: The aggregate subsidy on the different foods is 0.5 percent of GDP.
Source: Williamson Gray (1982).

incomes is to give them a small ration of fertilizer at no charge. Another way is to provide public services at less than full cost. This can be a deliberate part of food security policy rather than a regrettable outcome as long as a large share of the unrecovered costs goes to increase the incomes of the target group.

Why not simply give the target population cash? This makes sense if it is difficult and costly to convey added purchasing power by other means. If it

---

Box 3-5. The Arithmetic of Cost-Effectiveness in Public Works

A simple example shows how sensitive the cost-effectiveness of public works programs is to the wage and type of program. Assume that a program begins in a region in which 1,000 households subsist on an average of $1 a day and other households earn in excess of $2 a day. The objective is to raise household income of the first group to a least $2 a day. Further assume that working in the program costs participants 50 cents a day out-of-pocket for added food, travel to and from work, and so forth. A wage of $2.50 would then be enough to attract the target population and keep away other workers who earn more than $2 a day. If the value of a day's work performed under the program is $2.50 and it costs $3.50 for wages and materials, the public cost of augmenting incomes is $1. For each dollar spent on the program, the target population's income would increase by $1. If the value of a day's work were $3, each dollar spent on augmenting income would increase the target population's income by $2. Clearly, this program would be cost-effective.

Public works programs rarely achieve this cost-effectiveness. In many cases they create assets of low value. In the example above, if the value of a day's work were $1 rather than $2.50, it would cost the state $2.50 for each dollar of income transferred to the target population. If the daily wage offered were $3.50 rather than $2.50, the program would attract many workers from outside the target population. It might then cost the state as much as $5 to $10 to augment the income of people in the target population by $1 a day.

Box 3-6. UNICEF's Cash Transfer Project in Ethiopia

Early in 1984 UNICEF set up a targeted cash transfer pilot project in Ethiopia. Initially about 2,000 poor families in the Gonder and Shoa regions received $17 a month. In return for this cash transfer those who were physically able contributed labor to a range of local employment schemes, such as building roads and small-scale irrigation facilities. Now the project has been expanded to benefit at least 7,000 families in Ethiopia and is to be replicated in Burkina Faso. A sliding scale has also been introduced so that the amount of cash each household receives depends on family size.

It is more politically palatable to transfer food than cash. However, when famine is not the result of an overall shortage of food but the result of certain households suffering a temporary loss of income or losing their ability to produce food, a cash transfer enables people to purchase food in local or neighboring markets. In such situations cash transfers are more cost-effective than the provision of food, are easier to administer, and reach the affected population more quickly.

In Ethiopia UNICEF estimated the average cost of transporting a ton of grain from the port to drought areas such as the Gonder and Shoa regions to be $130. By providing cash rather than food, UNICEF enabled households to acquire the equivalent amount of food at a much lower cost to the government. Cash also enables households to purchase items other than food, such as medicines and seeds, that are vital for survival or that are important if households are to reestablish themselves as independent producers. Moreover, the program also indirectly helped the local farmers to sell their food surpluses. The success of the UNICEF cash transfer project is indicated in the results of a survey taken in Menz, which suggests that malnutrition has declined among children living in project areas.

Obviously, the national aggregate demand for food increases whether households are given cash or food transfers. To satisfy this increase in demand, either more food needs to be produced or food imports are required. This case merely illustrates that when food is available in rural areas, it is highly cost-ineffective to ship marketed surpluses from the rural regions of a country to its cities while sending food aid in the opposite direction.

Box 3-7. Types of Intervention to Reduce Chronic Food Insecurity

Type I—Illustrative of Many Countries in Sub-Saharan Africa

In these countries the highest priority must be given to improving food security by developing the agricultural sector, since most of the poor derive their income and most of the food they consume from farming. Strengthening agriculture under these circumstances can also have beneficial effects for the urban poor, although this will depend on the means used.

When most of the people facing chronic food insecurity produce internationally traded agricultural commodities—food or nonfood—the first task is to determine whether the prices are below border prices because of price controls or unrealistic exchange rates. Lifting these prices to world levels promotes economic growth generally and food security for many of the rural poor. The choice of compensatory policies to protect the net buyers of food—the landless and the urban poor—largely depends on the fiscal and administrative requirements of the different options. Subsidizing the retail price of some centrally processed foods can be cost-effective if the intended target population is dispersed. If the consumption of processed food (such as flour) is not widespread and the poor are concentrated, however, other interventions become important, such as employment programs for landless groups and food subsidies for the urban poor.

In many Type I countries, raising agricultural prices will not do enough to improve rural incomes. Public investments in infrastructure are also needed to reduce production and marketing costs and to improve research and extension programs to raise productivity. Unlike interventions that raise food prices, investments in infrastructure will not reduce—and can even raise—the real income of net food buyers, especially when the output of nontradable foods is increased.

Some of the people facing chronic food insecurity produce food that is not internationally traded, particularly in isolated regions of large countries, in which transport costs or food habits isolate food prices from international prices. Their real incomes can be increased only by subsidizing output or inputs or by providing infrastructure. Again, the best interventions are those that can be targeted and have few efficiency costs. Emphasis should be given to subsidizing inputs or infrastructure that already have a high rate of return on conventional economic grounds.

Type II—Illustrative of Several Countries in Latin America

If the urban poor predominate, ways should be found to bring down the prices to consumers without lowering them to producers—that is, without taxing food producers. The costs of these ways should be explored before moving on to any other policy that would discriminate against food producers. If fiscal and administrative resources are scarce, prices might be lowered by subsidizing imports. This clearly taxes agriculture and involves an efficiency loss that can be large, so specific foods should be chosen to minimize that loss. But marketwide consumer subsidies of selected foods are relatively efficient if centrally processed foods figure heavily in the diets of the poor and not in those of the rich, and if the poor are dispersed. If not, targeted programs may be more efficient: they have fewer leakages to unintended groups, but they are much more difficult to administer.

Type III—Illustrative of Such Countries as India and Bangladesh

When the food-insecure are widely distributed throughout society and consist of the landless, the urban poor, and subsistence farmers with little marketed surplus, the choice of an appropriate mix of policy instruments is more complicated. Low food prices clearly benefit the urban poor, but they have no effect on subsistence farmers and an ambiguous effect on the landless. The most suitable policies—those that have low tradeoffs with efficiency—would combine employment programs for the landless, subsidized inputs and investments in infrastructure for subsistence farmers, and targeted food programs for the urban poor. Such packages can be very costly, and their success depends on efficient administration and effective targeting in urban and rural areas.

An alternative is to try to identify marketwide policies that would help the landless and urban poor at a lower fiscal cost and with few losses in efficiency. This might be done through import policies that lower the prices of foods heavily consumed by the urban poor and the landless and that do not strongly affect the employment prospects of the landless. This has been done for wheat in India. In other words, the landless must gain from the lower prices more than what they might lose in employment. These policies will have to be complemented by targeted subsidies to subsistence farmers.

costs $2, $3, or $5 to transfer a dollar of income through public employment schemes or other income transfer programs, cash payments may be more cost-effective (see Box 3-6).

Marketwide Interventions

Because it is difficult to reach a rural target population and because the cost of delivering income transfer payments in kind is high, it is tempting to provide income transfers to a population group at large—say, to all users of fertilizer, to all producers of cotton or wheat, or to all users of irrigation water in a river basin. Such interventions include subsidized prices for fertilizer, import quotas or taxes on imported agricultural commodities, subsidy payments for agricultural exports, and public investment programs in sectors that fail to meet the criterion of economic return applied to other sectors.

These marketwide interventions, however, are highly cost-ineffective ways of augmenting the incomes of people facing chronic food insecurity. The full economic costs of these programs often far exceed the income transferred because of the efficiency losses. Moreover, much of the income transferred goes not to the target group but to the large-scale farmer, since the benefits of such subsidies accrue in proportion to the amount purchased or sold. Also, marketwide interventions to augment the incomes of suppliers often have the added disadvantage of either raising prices of important items in the consumption basket of those whose incomes are not augmented or raising prices of the unsubsidized inputs they need to make a living.

Interventions in Different Conditions

This chapter has focused on the effectiveness of individual policies in reaching a target group. Yet most countries have a variety of target groups and a wide range of circumstances, which call for a package of policies. Appropriate packages will differ greatly, depending on the conditions and situation of each country. Box 3-7 provides some examples of possible interventions in three broad types of country.

4

National Measures to Reduce Transitory Food Insecurity

It is possible to reduce both transitory food insecurity and the instability of food prices. There is enough food in the world to feed everyone, and the financial means exist to help people out of temporary economic and agricultural crises. Not only can this assistance be offered, moreover, but it is highly desirable to do so for several very good reasons.

Temporary sharp reductions in a population's ability to produce or purchase food and other essentials undermine long-term development and cause loss of human and physical capital from which it may take years to recover. Reduced purchasing power can cause undernutrition, which strips rural households of the energy needed to grow next year's crop and of the means to send children to school. Some families may never recover lost seeds, cattle, and implements. When small farmers are forced to sell their land, income disparities increase, and the social organization of production may deteriorate. The resulting disruptions in family structure also make it difficult to maintain minimum health standards.

Although temporary sharp rises in food prices do not cause nutritional deficiencies for most people—usually they have enough income or savings to see them through such crises—unstable food prices can also create political instability and long-term social tension. The politically strong often engineer compensatory wage increases, which, by benefitting a select few, exacerbate inequitable income distribution.

Finally, growing evidence shows that agricultural output, particularly from small farmers with little accumulated wealth and limited access to credit, would expand more rapidly if these farmers could be assured of having a more stable income from sale of their produce. They are the least able to adopt modern production methods that offer higher potential but are often risky.

The major sources of transitory food insecurity are year-to-year variations in international food prices, foreign exchange earnings, domestic food production, and household incomes. These often are related. In competitive national markets the price of food is determined by supply (domestic production, imports, and changes in stocks) and demand (domestic demand plus exports). Fluctuations in these variables and the correlations between them influence the stability of both domestic food prices and consumption.

Countries can generally do little about unstable international food prices and the terms of trade in the world markets. And the international community, despite intensive efforts for many years, has not been able to do much to reduce this instability. Therefore, this chapter focuses on policies that stabilize domestic food prices by stabilizing the domestic supply and demand of food. What can developing countries do to reduce fluctuations in their domestic food prices? What kinds of international initiatives can help? And what can be done to prevent transitory food insecurity when it is caused by a severe drop in income or by local declines in food production after such catastrophies as droughts or floods?

Stabilizing the Domestic Food Supply

A nation's food supply can be stabilized by stabilizing domestic production, by buffer stocks, or by trade. Not all options are always open, but when options exist, cost-effectiveness should be the main criterion.

Two questions arise: how much should the domestic food supply be stabilized, and what measures can achieve this desired stabilization at the least cost? The answer to the first question depends partly on the costs involved and partly on the government's judgment of the benefits from greater stability. This judgment is necessarily subjective, and little formal advice can be given. Governments should note, however, that food security does not require a stable supply or price for every food. It often is feasible and cheaper to compensate for a shortfall in the supply of one food by increasing the supply of another.

Stabilizing Domestic Production

Domestic production can be stabilized through investments in drainage, irrigation, and pest or disease control. Such investments may be justified by comparing their expected costs and benefits (excluding the benefits of stabilization per se). But is it sensible to make such investments merely for the sake of stabilization? It is not when the food concerned is internationally traded. In that case it is more effective to stabilize the domestic supply by adjusting imports or exports. If a food is not tradable and is perishable (such as milk, tubers, root crops, and fresh vegetables), however, stabilizing production is the only option, for neither trade nor storage is feasible. The only choice is then between different methods and degrees of stabilizing production. If trade is constrained merely by the high cost of transferring the food to and from an area, the supply can be stabilized by developing a transport infrastructure to cut this cost. The choice between investing in transport infrastructure or in production stabilization should be determined by cost-effectiveness.

Many other cases fall between these extremes. For instance, in Brazil imports can augment the supply of the edible beans preferred by consumers. But international trade in such beans is small, so that additional imports could only partially compensate for fluctuations in production. Buffer stocks can be maintained, however, because beans are not highly perishable. The key consideration in this case is whether measures to stabilize bean production are more cost-effective than buffer stocks.

Stabilizing with Buffer Stocks

Developing buffer stocks of food in plentiful years for use in lean years is the most commonly advocated method for stabilizing domestic supplies. Buffer stocks can, in principle, achieve any level of stability. The technology of storing grain is also well established. But even fairly large stocks cannot completely eliminate instability of supply, and the cost of maintaining buffer stocks to achieve a high level of stabilization tends to be quite high. Moreover, as the size of the operation increases, a buffer stock's marginal benefit decreases and its marginal cost rises sharply. There are several reasons for this outcome.

- Buffer stocks, to be effective, must be stored for several years.
- Amortization costs of the storage facility must also be borne in years when it is not used.
- Excess supplies often cannot be stored because of limited storage space.
- Stocks are often unavailable because they have not been accumulated or have already been used.

As a result, small buffer stocks may be an economic way to provide some stability. If a high degree of stability is sought, however, large buffer stocks are unlikely to be cost-effective compared with the cost of a flexible trade policy (see Box 4-1).

Whether buffer stocks are financially viable depends on how much their high operating costs are offset by gains in stabilizing food supplies. Such gains, in turn, depend largely on how much a country avails itself of the opportunity to stabilize the domestic price through trade. If trade is precluded, the size of the gains will depend mainly on the elasticity of demand; the more inelastic the demand, the higher the gap between the cost of acquiring the stock and the price for which it can be sold.

Box 4-1. The High Cost of Buffer Stocks

The cost and degree of stabilization resulting from buffer stocks of different sizes and operated under different storage rules are illustrated in Box Table 4-1A and Box Figures 4-1A and 4-1B. These results are based on a dynamic-stochastic simulation model in which production is assumed to follow a normal distribution. Details on the methodology are presented in the note to the table.

Two storage rules are contrasted. Under storage rule A, any production above the mean is stored until storage capacity is reached; any production short of the mean is supplemented from stocks in storage. Under storage rule B, stocks go into storage only if production exceeds 110 percent of mean production, and stocks are withdrawn only if production falls below 90 percent of the mean.

For buffer stocks of all sizes, the standard deviation of supply is less under rule A than under rule B. In addition, the cost of each ton stored is lower under rule A, although the probability of the domestic supply being far above or far below the mean is lower under rule B. Under rule A, the average cost for each ton of stored grain ranges from $53 with the lower storage capacity (higher turnover) to $133 with the higher storage capacity. Under rule B the cost per ton of stored grain varies from $89 to $271. As the size of the buffer stock is increased, the additional amount of grain stored per unit of storage capacity sharply declines. The marginal storage cost per ton of grain therefore sharply rises. Under rule A the marginal cost ranges from $53 to $313. Under rule B the marginal cost of storing a ton of grain is $584 when the storage capacity is 400,000 tons.

For the first 50,000 tons of storage capacity under storage rule B, the chance of supply shortages (supplies less than 90 percent of the mean) drops from 16 to 9 percent. Increasing the storage capacity from 100,000 to 200,000 tons decreases the chance of a similar supply shortfall from 4.6 to 1.5 percent (see Box Figure 4-1A). The marginal annual cost for each 1 percent reduction in the chance of a shortfall increases from $86,000 for the first 50,000 tons to $2.5 million when the storage capacity is increased from 250,000 to 300,000 tons (see Box Figure 4-1B).

Now consider the possible cost of achieving stabilization through trade. To illustrate, assume that a country is a net importer of grain in years of both good and bad grain harvests. This country has the option of stabilizing food supplies by importing less in some years and more in others. The money thus saved from importing less grain in a good harvest year needs to be invested in short-term financial instruments to ensure sufficient funds to offset production

Box Figure 4-1A. Probability of the Grain Supply Falling below 90 Percent of the Mean, at Varying Levels of Stock Storage Capacity (Storage Rule B)

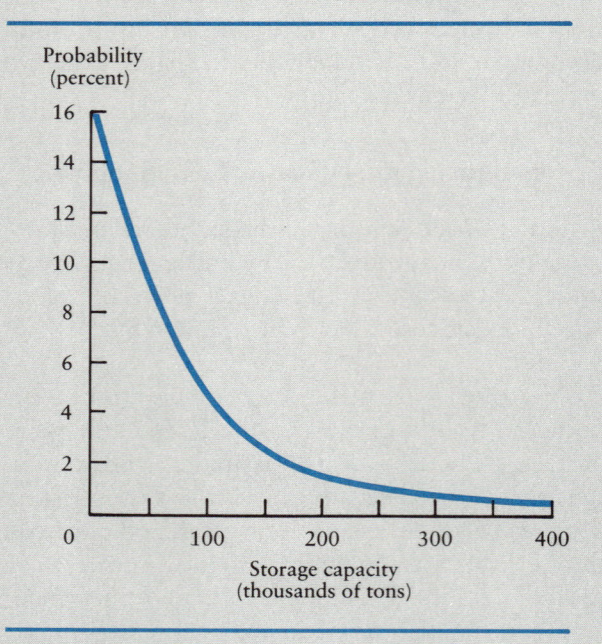

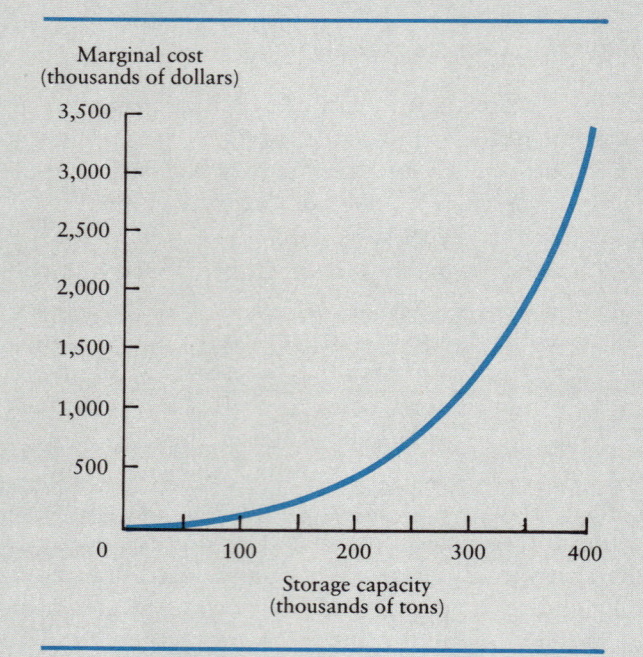

Box Figure 4-1B. Marginal Annual Cost of Changing by 1 Percent the Probability of the Grain Supply Falling below 90 Percent of the Mean, at Varying Levels of Stock Storage Capacity (Storage Rule B)

Box Table 4-1A. Expected Costs and Stabilization Effects of Different Buffer Stocks

Storage capacity (thousands of tons)	Standard deviation of supply (thousands of tons)	Probability of supply being less than 900,000 tons (percent)	Annualized storage cost (thousands of dollars)	Expected amount of grain stored (thousands of tons)	Expected average storage cost (dollars per ton)	Expected marginal storage cost (dollars per ton)
0	100	15.9	—	—	—	—
Storage rule A						
50	84	11.6	665	12.5	53	53
100	73	8.8	1,288	20.8	62	75
200	61	5.8	2,478	29.9	83	131
400	48	4.1	5,078	38.2	133	313
Storage rule B						
50	88	9.0	596	6.7	89	89
100	83	4.6	1,176	10.8	109	141
200	77	1.5	2,473	15.3	162	288
400	72	0.5	5,829	21.0	271	584

—Not applicable.
Note: Production is assumed to follow a normal distribution, with a mean of 1 million tons and standard deviation of 100,000 tons. The results are based on a dynamic-stochastic simulation model, in which 6,000 production events are drawn at random from an assumed normal probability distribution with a mean of 1 million tons and a coefficient of variation of 10 percent of the mean. The sequentially ordered production events are allocated into 200 thirty-year samples. The storage activity in any particular year is determined by the level of production in the current year, but withdrawals cannot exceed the available supply in storage, and additions to the stock cannot exceed the unused storage capacity. The cost of holding supplies in storage depends on the length of time the stock is held in storage and on the value of the commodity. In the case used for illustration, the commodity is valued at $200 per ton. The assumed annual variable storage cost is $20 per ton (including interest on inventory, deterioration of the stock, and so forth), the annual amortization cost is approximately $9 per ton of storage capacity, and the loading and unloading cost is $5 per ton.

Box Table 4-1B. Financial Gain from Different Sizes of Buffer Stock Operations in the Absence of Trade

Storage capacity (thousands of tons)	Low elasticity of demand[a] — Annualized net revenue from stock (thousands of dollars)	Low elasticity of demand[a] — Net revenue per ton of grain released (dollars per ton)	High elasticity of demand[a] — Annualized net revenue from stock (thousands of dollars)	High elasticity of demand[a] — Net revenue per ton of grain released (dollars per ton)
Storage rule A				
50	81	6	−168	−13
100	−429	−20	−706	−33
200	−1,696	−53	−1,896	−60
400	−4,128	−100	−4,322	−107
Storage rule B				
50	24	−4	−199	−30
100	−370	−34	−643	−61
200	−1,131	−76	−1,768	−120
400	−4,102	−197	−4,499	−218

Note: See the notes to Box Table 4-1A. Two demand elasticities are assumed—one very elastic, the other not. The financial gain of buying low and selling high exceeds the cost of storage only at the lowest stock level (50,000 tons) under storage rule A, and then only if demand is inelastic. In all other cases storage costs exceed the gains.
a. A kinked linear demand function is used. For the low elasticity case, the elasticities are 0.2 and 0.3 at the mean price ($200 per ton) for the left and right segments, respectively, of the demand function. For the high elasticity case, the corresponding elasticities are 0.3 and 0.5.

shortfalls in a year when higher imports are required.

The cost of doing this would be the difference in the rate of interest earned from the short-run financial instrument and the rate of return on longer-term investments. If this difference is, say, 3 percent a year, if good and bad harvests are on average five years apart, and if the price of imported grain is $200 a ton, then the cost of stabilizing the supply would be $32 a ton. If stabilizing a country's grain supply requires exports in some years and imports in others, the cost of using trade might increase to $100 a ton to account for the difference between the FOB and CIF grain price. Although the cost of stabilizing supply through trade increases only slightly with higher levels of stabilization, the cost of doing so with a buffer stock rises steeply.

The result is that a small degree of supply stabilization is likely to cost less or only marginally more by using a buffer stock than by flexible trading. High levels of stabilization, however, will likely cost much less with a flexible trade policy than with buffer stocks. Box Table 4-1B shows the net revenue from operating a buffer stock under the previously cited conditions, except with variable grain prices.

If trade is used to stabilize price completely, and the international price is stable or the accumulation and withdrawal of stocks is governed by the size of domestic harvests, there are no financial gains to offset the cost of a buffer stock operation. If storage decisions are triggered by changes in international prices, however, there would be some financial gains to offset storage costs, although these gains can be expected to be less than the gains realized from a buffer stock operated under a scenario that precludes all trade.

The financial gain from storing grain when the price is low and reselling it when the price is high generally exceeds the cost of storage only if stock levels are relatively low and then only if demand is inelastic. In most cases storage costs exceed the gains, even though the stock is sold from storage at a higher price than it was originally bought for. In other words, the net revenue from the resale is still negative. Thus, only under certain circumstances would there be incentives for private buffer stocks, and any larger stocks would have to be operated as a public utility.

Stabilizing through Trade

Trade can help most countries to stabilize the domestic food supply at the least cost. Yet few developing countries fully appreciate the potential cost-effectiveness of trade or sufficiently use it as an instrument of stabilization. Advocating the use of trade to stabilize the domestic food supply does not imply a particular rate of protection—whether negative, zero, or positive. A constant tariff, for instance, affects average domestic production, consumption, and price, but it generally does not affect the stability of the domestic price. There are, of course, exceptions. For example, a high enough tariff could eliminate trade (importing or exporting) in all circumstances, while a low tariff would not hamper trade. With the high tariff the stability of the domestic price would then depend on the relative stability of domestic supply and demand. With the low tariff (and under a free trading regime) the domestic price would fluctuate with the international price. Whether the domestic price would be more stable with or without trade in this case is an empirical question.

The use of trade for stabilization is not the same as instituting a free trading regime. It would be the same only if international prices were stable and domestic prices, in the absence of trade, were always above import prices or below export prices. As was already noted, however, the relative stability in international food prices during the 1950s and 1960s is not likely to return. Moreover, the instability of border prices in domestic currency may be even greater than that in foreign currency because of fluctuations in exchange rates. In addition, large fluctuations in demand and supply can be expected to cause many countries to trade in some years but not in others. For most countries, then, a free trading regime is not likely to assure domestic food price stability, although it may help to reduce instability.

Governments can stabilize the domestic food price to any desired extent by allowing the value of imports or exports to vary. In general, this is best accomplished by variable levies on trade, such as subsidies or taxes on the price of the imported commodity. In the past many governments chose to license variable amounts of imports or exports rather than to stabilize food prices through variable levies. In principle there is no reason why the domestic food supply cannot be stabilized in this way. In practice, however, it is highly unlikely that a central authority can acquire the considerable amount of added information about domestic supply, demand, and price conditions needed for direct rather than indirect intervention. And despite their best intentions to stabilize food prices, government agencies often bow to competing demands for fiscal resources and pressures from special interest groups. Whether intentionally or not, quantitative trade interventions may aggravate rather than reduce instability in domestic food prices.

Differences between domestic and international prices can be maintained only to the extent that they are smaller than the differences between prices at home and in neighboring countries. If not, there will be an incentive to export or import the commodity. For example, if an import subsidy drops a nation's domestic price below the price in a neighboring country, the subsidy will support not only the imports entering the domestic market but also the imports diverted to the neighboring country. When the domestic price is set above the international price, it is necessary to tax all potential imports of that commodity. If the flow of commodities coming across the borders from neighboring countries cannot be taxed, it will not be possible to achieve the goal of stabilization.

When import prices and domestic food supplies are unstable, the stabilization of domestic food prices through trade could result in highly unstable demand for foreign exchange from the food sector. Countries will then be required to hold larger reserves of foreign exchange or to use financial instruments. These financial instruments are not costless, but in most cases they are likely to cost much less than large buffer stocks. Several international initiatives to help countries cope with the financial instability associated with stabilizing domestic prices through trade are discussed in Chapter 5.

Stabilizing Domestic Demand

Unstable demand is typical in countries that get much of their income from agriculture or whose income depends on volatile export prices. In such cases stable domestic food prices will not stabilize consumption.

If the main cause of unstable household income is unstable export prices, a price equalization fund may be the answer. For instance, if much of a population's income depends on the price of sugar, coffee, or copper, the government could impose an export tax on these commodities when the world price is high, provide an export subsidy when the world price is low, or vary tax rates accordingly. If the supply is elastic and the country is a major supplier of the commodity to the world market, such a policy would destabilize the world price and might, therefore, require a very large fund to equalize prices. If many countries are stabilizing the domestic price of an export commodity—especially at great cost to themselves—a commodity agreement or supply controls and buffer stocks may be needed. But reaching consensus on a commodity agreement is not easy.

If the main cause of unstable income (and food demand) is random fluctuations in agricultural production, crop insurance is one remedy, but few such schemes have been successful, and they also tend to be very costly. Other possible measures include diversifying products, creating public employment schemes, making credit easier to obtain, and allowing flexible terms on credit payment.

Protecting Vulnerable Population Groups

Many countries may not be willing or able to stabilize domestic food prices. Moreover, it may not always be desirable to do so. For example, when a country is struck by a poor harvest, a rise in food prices may be needed to sustain farmers' incomes. In this situation even stable prices will not protect everyone against transitory food insecurity. Personal incomes, not just aggregate incomes, also need to be stabilized. Any measures to protect vulnerable groups must assure them of a minimum level of real income when prices for food rise above normal or when incomes drop temporarily.

If the vulnerable group is small and easily identifiable, effective government interventions can be targeted to reach them at a reasonable cost. If the real income of these people falls below a minimum level because of a temporary rise in food prices, food rations can compensate. The ration need not consist of the foods whose prices have risen, but the value of the ration (at market prices) should be high enough to compensate for the rise in the prices of the foods these people consume.

If the vulnerable group is large, it would be expensive and administratively difficult to set up targeted programs to augment incomes. In this case stabilizing the price of the staple food would be more feasible and the fiscal burden to the government much lower. Domestic producers would bear much of the cost if a large share of the country's supply were produced domestically.

Price stabilization is not the solution, however, if the target population's real income falls because of either a temporary drop in employment or a drop in the amount of commodities it produces. After a drought or flood, targeted income programs, such as free food rations and employment programs, are clearly needed.

Large global or national buffer stocks are often suggested as a way to prevent famines. In many situations, however, it would be much less costly to store financial resources from one period to the next. They could then be made available to people as needed. If the transfer of financial resources is not feasible or if local supplies are depleted, victims of famine may need to be given food at a concessional price or even at no cost. Even then the food need not come from buffer stocks, because the cost of stored food might well greatly exceed its market price when it is needed.

Although countries need to consider alternatives to buffer stocks for coping with temporary emergencies, there sometimes are political reasons for not doing so. Buffer stocks are a politically attractive way to save for a bad year—they are attractive to producers in developing countries and to donor countries with surplus production. Moreover, if low-income countries find it difficult to hold foreign exchange reserves or do not get clear assurances that donor countries will give aid in food emergencies, these low-income countries may have to consider stockpiling grain. This solution is obviously better than none, because governments derive political security from food stocks. Still, costly stockpiling is not always the answer.

Even though countries can ensure stable supplies by adjusting their food trade, they often lack the capability to get food where and when it is needed. To address this shortcoming, countries could improve their capability to move supplies more quickly and could also hold a minimum of strategically situated emergency food stocks to ensure adequate supplies until imports can be delivered.

Regional Schemes for Cooperation

Sometimes it is in the interest of several neighboring countries to join forces to stabilize their food supplies. Many regional cooperation schemes exist. Although the circumstances and objectives vary, they have several features in common. They all attempt to establish regional reserves of food, to facilitate interregional trade in food, to establish regional information networks about food, and to support improved food production efficiency through regional research centers.

To succeed, these schemes should meet at least three criteria. First, a region should contain both countries with a food surplus and countries with a food deficit—the countries should not be vulnerable to simultaneous crop failures. Second, an adequate storage, transport, and communication system should link the countries so food can flow between them. Third, the countries should have a high degree of political unity—perhaps the most important and most difficult precondition. Without agreement on domestic food policies, on emergency buffer stocks, and on sharing the financial burden, any regional scheme will dissolve. It is no surprise then that, except for the Association of South-East Asian Nations (ASEAN), no other regional association has set up emergency reserves, despite stated desires to do so. (The ASEAN reserve, which contains only 50,000 tons, has never been used.)

Even without emergency reserves, regional cooperation can promote food security. In agricultural research this is being done through the system supported by the Consultative Group on International Agricultural Research (CGIAR). More research is needed, however, on storage and processing technology. Formation of regional early-warning systems, with the FAO's assistance, will help ensure that food from aid or commercial imports will be available when and where it is needed. In Africa such an early-warning system is being set up through the Southern Africa Development Coordination Conference. In Asia a system is being set up with the help of Japan. By monitoring crops in the region, these systems can provide a base for more mutual assistance in emergencies. In 1979, for instance, India, Pakistan, and Tanzania gave substantial cereal loans to their neighbors, who saw this as a way to reduce both their need for foreign exchange and the political discomfort of depending on fluctuating supplies of food aid from traditional bilateral sources.

5
International Support for Food Security

Much foreign assistance for food security has been used to accelerate agricultural development and to increase food production. These are important aspects of the problem when they affect the real incomes of vulnerable consumers and producers. The progress in diminishing food insecurity has been disappointing, however, partly because of the widely held misperception that food shortages are the root of the problem. The disturbing fact is that food insecurity has become even worse in many countries, despite higher per capita food production.

Although far too many people eat too little, the energy deficit in their diets represents only a small part of the food energy consumed in most countries. Increasing the food supply would not eliminate this problem, since it would not necessarily improve the incomes and purchasing power of the poor. That is why international support should focus on policies and investments that would improve the distribution of benefits from economic growth by raising the real income of people facing chronic food insecurity and stabilizing the access to food for people facing transitory food insecurity.

The international community, in supporting food security, should be guided by the four most important conclusions of this report:

- The lack of food security is a lack of purchasing power of people and nations. Thus, there is a strong convergence between the objectives of alleviating poverty and increasing food security.

- Food security does not necessarily result from achieving food self-sufficiency in a country or from a rapid increase in food production, as desirable as those goals may be for other reasons.

- Food security in the long run is a matter of achieving economic growth and alleviating poverty. In the shorter run it is a matter of redistributing purchasing power and resources toward those who are undernourished. By choosing redistributive policies on the basis of cost-effectiveness, governments can do much to improve the food security of their people.

- Transitory food insecurity—which results from fluctuations in domestic harvests, international prices, and foreign exchange earnings—can best be reduced through measures that facilitate trade and provide income relief to afflicted people.

International donors—multilateral, bilateral, and private—should help countries shape long-term solutions and alleviate the distress from short-term emergencies. They should encourage the adoption of appropriate national policies and provide the external financing needed to promote national food security. They should also push for an international trading environment more conducive to worldwide food security.

Analysis and Advice

The main objective of analysis and advice given by international organizations is to help countries pursue cost-effective interventions to increase food security. How much governments will or should spend on food security measures depends on national priorities, the size of the problem, and the availability of fiscal and administrative resources. Even when political, budgetary, and bureaucratic forces constrain the choices, external advice can help improve the cost-effectiveness of interventions to promote food security.

The first steps in determining a cost-effective program are to identify the size and characteristics of the vulnerable population groups as well as the sources of instability in food production, prices, and incomes. Such an evaluation should differentiate between chronic and transitory food insecurity, because they require different policies. Donors need to support the development of analytical capabilities to make such evaluations, since these capabilities are often lacking in developing countries. Donors should also coordinate their work and have a common perception of the problems and potential remedies of food insecurity.

There are three major policy options to promote food security. *Policies to promote growth with equity* might include accelerating public investments in agriculture and in the human capital of the poor and eliminating distortions that inhibit growth and discriminate against the poor (such as taxes on labor-intensive products and subsidies for capital inputs). *Policies to augment the incomes of the chronically vulnerable population* could include well-targeted income or food transfers, which may involve high administrative costs but hold down fiscal costs and efficiency losses; general consumer subsidies on selected basic staple foods, which have high fiscal costs but are easy to implement and do not distort producer prices; and import subsidies, which are easy to implement and have low fiscal costs but distort producer prices and may therefore have large efficiency losses. *Policies to alleviate transitory food insecurity* include stabilizing domestic food prices primarily through trade and financial measures, holding emergency stocks and introducing other contingency measures to ensure adequate food supplies, and safeguarding minimum incomes of vulnerable populations through relief measures, especially when there is a sharp temporary decline in income.

External Finance

International efforts to promote food security should proceed in four directions: emphasize lending operations that promote growth and benefit the poorest people; increase the use of trade finance and other international financing arrangements for alleviating transitory food insecurity; integrate food aid with financial aid; and make a stronger commitment to coordinating aid, which would enhance the effectiveness of individual donor efforts. Most important, development agencies should regard the promotion of food security as an integral part of the development effort. They should not only support economic growth and direct measures to reduce chronic food insecurity but also involve themselves in efforts to prevent disruptions in the ability of people to feed themselves, to educate their young, and to maintain good health. These disruptions can have long-lasting effects on the development of human capital by attenuating health and cognitive skills.

Lending to Reduce Poverty and Chronic Food Insecurity

An important objective of financial aid should be to alleviate chronic food insecurity through investments and appropriate institutional and policy changes. Financial assistance should support cost-effective policies to raise the income of the most disadvantaged groups and to secure them a minimum real income at all times. Bilateral and multilateral aid donors should continue to emphasize the need for accelerating economic growth in countries receiving external finance.

Financing investments that directly raise incomes of the poor should receive high priority. The best example is the priority given to raising the productivity and incomes of small-scale farmers as well as to creating increased employment opportunities in urban and rural areas. In addition, priority should be given to investments that increase food supplies and reduce food prices in countries or regions in which the people who face chronic food insecurity are net food buyers. Such investments could be in research to reduce production costs and in infrastructure to reduce marketing costs where this would lead to lower food prices. External finance should also support projects that cost-effectively distribute income in kind, for example, food or fertilizer rations at less-than-market prices to poor households. Providing the poor with access to preventive health services, nutrition education, drinking water, special foods for children, and the means for controlling family size are also important activities (Berg 1981; World Bank 1984).

Alleviating Transitory Food Insecurity

There are three main ways that external finance should help countries reduce transitory food insecurity: by ensuring the financial capacity to import enough food in years when food harvests are poor, international food prices are above normal, or foreign exchange earnings plummet; by increasing the capacity of their marketing systems; and by financing temporary relief to populations struck by natural or man-made disasters.

Commercial imports are usually available to any country that can pay the price (although food aid may be refused on political grounds at any time); a financial insurance scheme could ensure food supplies as needed. After much discussion and research on how best to stabilize food supplies (Reutlinger 1977; Goreux 1980; and Huddleston and Konandreas 1981), the International Monetary Fund modified in 1981 its Compensatory Financing Facility (CFF) to give countries financial assistance to ease transitory food insecurity (see Box 5-1). The cost of running such a facility is relatively small, and the logistics are simple. The purchase and delivery of the food under the scheme can be integrated with other food imports—something that is particularly important because the

---

Box 5-1. Financing for Fluctuating Cereal Import Costs

In 1981 the International Monetary Fund (IMF) set up an innovative scheme to finance grain imports for its member countries. The plan makes temporary financing available when a crisis, such as a crop failure or a surge in international grain prices, hits a member country with a balance of payments deficit.

The IMF decided to integrate this plan with its Compensatory Financing Facility (CFF), which helps countries troubled by fluctuations in their export earnings. Under the cereal import plan, the amount of financing available for the necessary extra imports is calculated as the difference between the cost of these imports during the most recent twelve months and the estimated average cost of cereal imports for five years, centered on the year the request is made. The excess cost of cereal imports is then either offset by extra export earnings or increased by an export shortfall from a rise or fall in average export earnings. To make financing timely, the plan allows early drawings.

Members may still use the CFF for export shortfalls alone, as they have in the past, or they may request funds on the basis of their excess import costs plus their export losses. If they choose the latter formula, they must use it in all requests for the ensuing three years.

The limit is 83 percent of a country's quota in the fund (the same as the limit for financing export shortages). For financing requests to cover both extra imports and export shortages, there is a joint limit of 105 percent. The current finance charge is 7 percent a year, plus a one-time service charge of 0.5 percent. The repayment period is five years.

The conditions for financing cereal imports are the same as for the CFF program. The excess cost of cereal imports should be temporary (reversible in a few years). Its causes should be largely beyond the control of the member country. The IMF must be satisfied that the member has a balance of payments need and that it will cooperate with the IMF in efforts to solve the balance of payments problems. To obtain financing that raises a member's drawings above 50 percent of its quota, the IMF must be satisfied that the member has been finding solutions to its balance of payments difficulties.

Since the beginning of the Cereal Import Scheme in 1981, there have been eleven drawings (three by Malawi, two each by Korea and Bangladesh, and one each by Kenya, Ghana, Jordan, and Morocco). They total SDR963 million (the value of the SDR on May 14, 1985 was $1). Of this, SDR394 million went to cover excess import costs and SDR569 million to cover shortfalls in export earnings.

The plan so far may have found only rather limited use for several reasons: declining cereal prices since 1981; relatively easy access to food aid; conditions attached to the import financing, including the short repayment period; and difficulty in providing the necessary data. In May 1985 the IMF reviewed the cereal facility and decided to extend it on existing terms for another four years.

amount of food needed to stabilize food supplies could be small in some years and large in others. Since buffer stocks—another way of stabilizing the national food supply—are costly by comparison, countries should usually be advised to avail themselves of credit from the CFF or make other arrangements to assure themselves of import financing when the need arises. This recommendation presumes that the CFF's capacity to ensure flexible financing of food imports for member countries will be maintained at its current level.

Ensuring a stable food supply requires more than financial capacity for flexible imports. A marketing system flexible enough to handle constantly varying amounts of food trade is also needed. Indeed, any improvement in marketing efficiency enhances food security by speeding delivery in emergencies and by reducing food prices to consumers without cutting prices to producers. Even if the marketing infrastructure can handle normal flows of food—and in many developing countries it cannot do so efficiently—few countries can handle large, sporadic increases in food imports and distribute them quickly and efficiently. To provide adequate food supplies until imports arrive, countries need strategically placed emergency food stocks—a worthy area for international support.

Food aid continues to be the main source of relief in famines. Because of tremendous improvements in transport and the flow of information in and among countries, the international community now plays a very important role in providing speedy relief during disasters. Better contingency planning could improve response times further and perhaps greatly increase efficiency in providing this relief. Early identification is essential, and adequate contingency planning for transport may be even more so. Other efforts to help vulnerable groups survive lean years might entail projects for crop diversification to reduce disaster risks or investments to improve transport under adverse circumstances.

Providing Food Aid

Food aid has long been the main way of helping low-income countries sustain domestic food supplies and protect the incomes of vulnerable groups against temporary shortfalls. The achievements in this area have been impressive. Few in favor of development aid would challenge this statement. But many would suggest that other forms of aid could be more efficient. This point is academic, however, because major donors will continue to make food aid an important part of their development assistance packages.

Food aid should be planned and managed with as much care as other forms of financial aid, but it often is not. What is the best way to use food aid in the interest of food security? Some new approaches should be considered.

For low-income countries with food deficits, food aid tends to be a large share of total aid, particularly nonproject aid, much of it in the form of budgetary support to recipient governments. One way to increase the effect of food aid and all other kinds of external finance on food security is for donors and national planners to reach a common understanding on the measures needed to improve long-term food security. Donors of both food and financial aid could then support consistent programs more strongly. One problem is that few donor institutions that administer food aid carry out the analytical tasks needed for such a dialogue. Combined efforts to bolster the capacity to do so, particularly among aid groups, would be more efficient and possibly more effective than individual attempts.

An increasing share of food aid is used to augment directly the incomes of the poor and their nutritional status. Much of this aid is administered by the World Food Programme and by such voluntary agencies as CARE and Catholic Relief Services. It often consists of co-financing for development projects provided in payments for work performed. Better integration of such projects with countries' overall development programs would greatly enhance the long-term benefits of such aid. Moreover, the efficiency of income transfers in many projects could be improved greatly if donors of food aid were to provide foods that have a high value to recipients relative to their delivered costs. In many instances, large gains could result from exchanging donated foods for money and providing recipients with foods locally available.

Food aid now does little to help countries cope with transitory food insecurity arising from higher food prices on the international market. Fixed budgets for food aid provide less food when prices are higher. Even worse, these budgets are often curtailed when prospects for commercial exports improve. Only a multiyear commitment by food aid donors, with flexible drawings in accord with a recipient country's needs, could make food aid a reliable instrument for relieving transitory food insecurity.

Coordinating Food Security Assistance

More effective coordination among donors in providing assistance to developing countries can avoid much of the misunderstanding, frustration, and wasted resources that have characterized past efforts. Some progress has been made in coordinating food aid, which in the past was frequently hampered by substantial information and managerial problems. For example, improvements in the Global Information and Early-Warning System in the Food and Agriculture Organization have resulted in more timely donor awareness of food supply shortfalls. In addition, the United Nations Development Programme has been instrumental in putting together interagency committees in several countries to monitor droughts.

Although coordination of aid has improved in recent years, the responsibility during regional or national food security emergencies too often belongs to everyone—and, therefore, to no one. Because coordination entails large costs in time and money, more efficient coordination—rather than simply more coordination—is needed. Every institution involved with food security issues will need to examine how it can help to improve this coordination. The World Bank will step up its involvement in the discussion of food security concerns among donors. For example, the matter will, where appropriate, be placed on the agenda at Consultative Group meetings.

International Trade

Improvements in worldwide transport, marketing, processing, and information have opened much greater opportunities for international trade in a large range of commodities including food. Trade contributes much to the food security of countries and households by increasing food supplies and augmenting employment and income. Two problems, however, have limited the benefits to food security from trade: trade restrictions and the growing instability in commodity prices and exchange rates. The international community can reduce these problems by advocating trade liberalization and by providing technical advice on how to cope with the fluctuating trading environment.

Tariffs, levies, and other restraints on trade have restricted markets for many exports from developing countries. This has reduced employment opportunities because many of the affected exports

---

Box 5-2. UNCTAD's Advisory Service for Procuring Food

Since 1978 UNCTAD has been operating a small-scale, low-cost procurement advisory service for developing countries that import food, especially those in Sub-Saharan Africa. The project, which is funded through the United Nations Development Programme and the government of Switzerland through June 1987, helps countries cut their food import costs by improving their purchasing systems, especially for grain imports.

Government staff responsible for procuring imports, especially in poor, small, landlocked countries, seldom have good knowledge of commercial practices in world grain markets. The project provides training in these practices to countries that want it. The project also makes evaluations and recommendations for increasing milling extraction rates, scheduling imports to keep freight costs down, choosing appropriate grades and varieties of cereals, and issuing contract tenders with fair, clear, and complete terms. Such technical reforms rarely require high-level political approval. Even so, minor changes in established practices are not always easy to introduce in government institutions, so project follow-up missions are often required.

An UNCTAD report estimates that savings from improved purchasing practices and broader knowledge of the market could be as high as 10 to 15 percent of the spending on food imports in developing countries—equivalent to $2 billion to $3 billion in 1982.

The advisory service also promotes economic cooperation among developing countries by assisting them with government-to-government trade contracts for rice. For example, Mauritania negotiated an 84,000 ton purchase of rice from the government of Thailand in 1983. The Thai price was $17.50 a ton lower than the lowest trade offer, for a saving of $1.5 million.

are in labor-intensive industries (such as textiles, vegetables, tobacco, and sugar) that often employ the poor. Although multilateral trade negotiations (under the auspices of the General Agreement on Trade and Tariffs) have produced significant advances toward more liberal trade relations, especially in manufactured products, trade restraints continue to have a detrimental effect on food security in developing countries. Restraints on trade do more than limit the opportunities for developing countries to earn income; they create more unstable commodity markets and thus contribute to transitory food insecurity. Persistent promotion of a more open trading system is therefore warranted.

Volatile exchange rates contribute to unstable national and international commodity markets. Foreign exchange markets would probably be more stable if domestic monetary and fiscal policies were more stable and if greater efforts were made to coordinate monetary and fiscal policies.

The policies of the major grain-trading countries on exchange rates and domestic prices cause much of the instability in the international price of food. The opportunities for fruitful multilateral action to resolve this instability are limited, however. The international community should therefore help food-insecure developing countries to use trade insurance mechanisms, say, by providing technical advice and support (see Box 5-2). Such advice could help developing countries use the tools of risk management (futures or options) that multinationals in developed countries already use.

The often-predicted Malthusian nightmare of population outstripping food production has never materialized. Instead, the world faces a narrower problem: many people do not have enough to eat, despite there being food enough for all. This is not a failure of food production, still less of agricultural technology. It is a failure to provide all people with the opportunity to secure enough food—something that is very hard to do in low-income countries. The roots of the predicament range from improper macroeconomic policies to the economic and political structures of local societies. The causes of food insecurity are complex and so are its remedies. The problem has been tackled successfully in some countries. This success can—and should—be repeated in many others.

Annex A

Methodologies

Estimating the Share of the Population with Chronically Inadequate Diets

The method for calculating the share of the population that consumes energy deficient diets can best be illustrated graphically. In Fig. A-1 the upper graph shows the relationship between income and energy in the daily diet; the lower graph shows the cumulative income distribution. Any standard of energy (shown on the vertical axis of the upper graph as Standard A or Standard B) implies a corresponding standard of income, below which people are expected to consume a daily diet containing less energy than indicated by the corresponding adequacy standard (shown on the horizontal axis of the lower graph as Y_a or Y_b).[1] The corresponding shares of the population that do not have enough income to consume diets with adequate energy are shown on the vertical axis of the lower graph.

Data on income distribution were available for only thirty-five countries, which contain about 70 percent of the population of all developing market economies.

For those countries the energy consumption function was estimated by allocating the total amount of energy in the national diet among the different income groups with the following equation:

$$C = a + b \sum w_i \ln X_i$$

where C is the energy (calories) content of each country's per capita food consumption (FAO

Figure A-1. Calculation of the Share of the Population with Energy-Deficient Diets

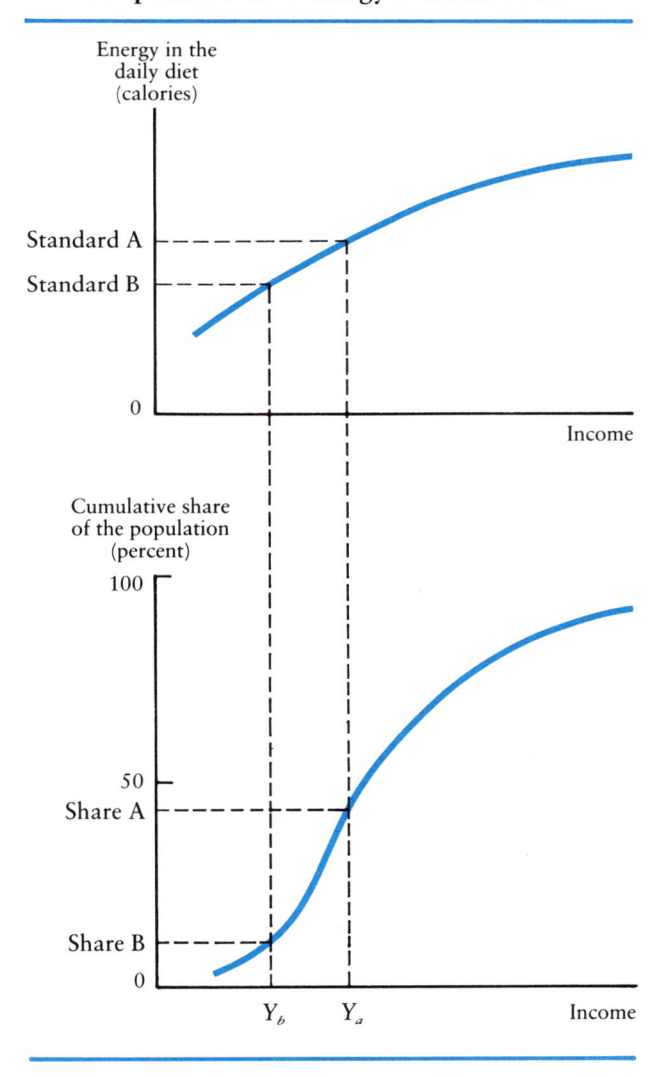

---

1. The two energy standards used correspond to 90 and 80 percent of country-specific FAO/WHO requirements. These are based on the caloric intake required to replace energy expenditure and to provide for growth in childhood. The requirements for populations were derived in two steps. First, the committee established requirements for a reference man and woman, who was assumed to be moderately active and whose weight and age were representative of groups whose food consumption and energy expenditure had been studied. Second, different requirement scales were constructed against these references on an individual country basis by accounting for observed demographic patterns in body weights, age, and sex structure. Data were taken from World Health Organization (1973).

55

Table A-1. Countries Included in the Estimation of Energy-Deficient Diets

Sub-Saharan Africa		Latin America and the Caribbean	
Benin	Mali	Argentina	Guyana
Botswana	Mauritania	Bahamas	Honduras*
Burkina Faso	Mauritius	Barbados	Jamaica*
Burundi	Mozambique	Bolivia	Mexico*
Cameroon	Niger	Brazil*	Nicaragua
Cape Verde	Nigeria	Chile*	Panama*
Central African Rep.	Rwanda	Colombia*	Paraguay
Chad	Senegal*	Costa Rica*	Peru*
Congo, People's Rep.	Sierra Leone	Dominican Republic*	Suriname*
Ethiopia	Somalia	Ecuador*	Trinidad and Tobago
Gabon*	Sudan*	El Salvador*	Uruguay*
Gambia, The	Swaziland	Guatemala*	Venezuela*
Ghana	Tanzania*		
Ivory Coast*	Togo		
Kenya*	Uganda		
Lesotho	Zaire		
Liberia	Zambia*		
Madagascar	Zimbabwe		
Malawi*			

East Asia and Pacific		South Asia	Middle East and North Africa	
Fiji		Afghanistan	Algeria	Morocco
Hong Kong		Bangladesh	Egypt	Syria
Indonesia*		Burma	Iran	Tunisia*
Korea, Rep. of*		India*	Iraq*	Turkey*
Malaysia*		Nepal	Jordan	Yemen Arab Republic
Papua New Guinea		Pakistan*	Lebanon	
Philippines*		Sri Lanka*		
Thailand*				

*Income distribution data were available for these thirty-five countries.

1980b), w_i is the share of the country population in the ith income group, and X_i is the average income of each group.[2] The parameter b is estimated with the equation:

$$b = \mu R$$

where μ is the energy income elasticity at the level at which food consumption equals per capita requirements, and R is the country-specific per capita energy requirement (FAO 1977). The energy-income elasticity at the level of energy adequacy was assumed to be 0.15 for all countries.

Estimates for fifty-five additional countries were made by extrapolating equations. The countries included in the estimation are listed in Table A-1. The equations were derived by regressing the shares of the population with energy-deficient diets in the thirty-five countries on the available energy in the average national diet and the energy requirement from the daily diet in each country (Equations (A-1) and (A-2) in Table A-2).

Changes in the shares of the population with energy deficient diets were calculated for each of the thirty-five countries with known income distributions on the assumption that the income distributions have remained unchanged. For the remaining fifty-five countries, the changes in the share of the population with energy-deficient diets were extrapolated by regressing the changes in the thirty-five countries on the changes in energy available in the national diet and energy requirements (Equations (A-3) and (A-4) in Table A-2).

Calculating the Approximate Efficiency of a Price Subsidy on Selected Foods

A first approximation of the income transfer efficiency of a subsidy, E^*, defined as the fraction of the subsidy reaching the target group can be made easily. It is the ratio of current per capita consumption of the particular food by the target

---

2. For a detailed description of the methodology see Reutlinger and Selowsky (1976).

Table A-2. Regressions Used for Extrapolations

$$(A\text{-}1) \quad Y_1 = 18.015 - 2.616\, X_1 + 0.00016\, Y_2 \qquad R^2 = 0.93$$
$$\phantom{(A\text{-}1) \quad Y_1 = 18.015\ } (-19.1) \quad\ \ (8.6)$$

$$(A\text{-}2) \quad Y_2 = 10.034 - 1.472\, X_1 + 0.00010\, X_2 \qquad R^2 = 0.78$$
$$\phantom{(A\text{-}2) \quad Y_2 = 10.034\ } (-9.7) \quad\ \ (4.7)$$

$$(A\text{-}3) \quad Y_3 = 0.136 - 9.976\, X_3 + 7.455\, X_4 \qquad R_2 = 0.82$$
$$\phantom{(A\text{-}3) \quad Y_3 = 0.136\ } (-8.3) \quad\ \ (2.8)$$

$$(A\text{-}4) \quad Y_4 = 0.010 - 8.144\, X_3 + 2.422\, X_4 \qquad R^2 = 0.94$$
$$\phantom{(A\text{-}4) \quad Y_4 = 0.010\ } (-13.9) \quad\ \ (1.0)$$

where:

Y_1 = log of the share of the population with energy-deficient diets during 1969–71 (90 percent of FAO/WHO requirements)

Y_2 = log of the share of the population with energy-deficient diets during 1969–71 (80 percent of FAO/WHO requirements)

Y_3 = log of the compound change in the share of the population with energy-deficient diets during 1970–80 (90 percent of requirements)

Y_4 = log of the compound change in the share of the population with energy-deficient diets during 1970–80 (80 percent of requirements)

X_1 = log of the per capita energy in diet during 1969–71

$X_2 = (X_1) \cdot$ (the per capita energy requirement in the diet)

X_3 = log of the compound change in the per capita energy of the diet during 1970–80

$X_4 = (X_3) \cdot$ (the per capita energy requirements in the diet).

Note: Values in parentheses are *t* statistics.

population to that of the total population, multiplied by the share of the target population in the total population, that is,

$$E^* = S(Q_t/Q)$$

where S is the share of the target population, Q_t is the target population's per capita consumption, and Q is the total population's per capita consumption.

A more precise estimate of the income transfer efficiency, E, also needs to take account of the additional food consumed by the targeted groups and the rest of the population in response to the subsidy, that is,

$$E = [(1 + ke_t)/(1 + ke)]E^*$$

where k is the percent reduction in the price of the food and e_t and e are the demand elasticities of the target population and the total population, respectively. When the supply of the commodity in question is not perfectly elastic, the income transfer efficiency also becomes a function of its supply elasticity.

Annex B

Data

The Global Food Supply

Table B-1. Growth Rates of Food Production, 1960–80
(average annual percentage change)

Region	Total 1960–70	Total 1970–80	Per capita 1960–70	Per capita 1970–80
World	2.7	2.3	0.8	0.5
Developing countries	2.9	2.8	0.4	0.4
Low income	2.6	2.2	0.2	−0.3
Middle income	3.2	3.3	0.7	0.9
Sub-Saharan Africa	2.6	1.6	0.1	−1.1
East Asia	2.8	3.8	0.3	1.4
South Asia	2.6	2.2	0.1	0.0
Middle East and North Africa	2.6	2.9	0.1	0.2
Southern Europe	3.2	3.5	1.8	1.9
Latin America and the Caribbean	3.6	3.3	0.1	0.6
Industrialized market economies	2.3	2.0	1.3	1.1
Centrally planned economies	3.2	1.7	2.2	0.9

Note: Production data are weighted by world export unit prices. Decade growth rates are based on midpoints of five-year averages, except that 1970 is the average for 1969–71.
Sources: FAO; World Bank, *World Development Report 1982*.

Table B-2. Growth Rates in Real International and Border Prices for Wheat, Rice, and Maize, 1970–83
(average annual percentage change)

Region and country	Wheat		Rice		Maize	
International price[a]	−1.77	(−0.09)	−1.32	(0.31)	−2.60	(−1.40)
Border price						
East Africa						
Kenya	−2.97	(−0.89)	−2.53	(−0.89)	−3.79	(−2.58)
Tanzania	−6.49	(−4.55)	6.07	(−4.55)	−7.28	(−6.17)
Zaire	−10.62	(−6.57)	−8.28	(−6.57)	−12.26	(−10.99)
Zambia	−2.22	(−0.26)	−1.77	(−0.26)	−3.05	(−1.96)
West Africa						
Ghana	−22.71	(−20.80)	−22.36	(20.49)	−23.37	(21.84)
Nigeria[c]	−8.94	(−6.95)	−7.23	(−5.28)	−10.34	(−8.84)
Senegal	−2.71	(−1.17)	−2.27	(−0.78)	−3.54	(−2.47)
Upper Volta	−1.95	(−0.32)	−1.51	(0.08)	−2.78	(−1.63)
East Asia and Pacific						
Indonesia	−4.13	(−2.54)	−3.69	(−2.16)	−4.94	(−3.82)
Korea, Rep. of	−2.57	(−0.71)	−2.13	(−0.32)	−3.40	(−2.02)
Philippines	−3.09	(−1.61)	−2.65	(−1.22)	−3.91	(−2.90)
Thailand	−2.79	(−1.29)	−2.35	(−0.90)	−3.61	(2.59)
South Asia						
Bangladesh[b]	11.08	(8.38)	7.32	(8.38)	11.05	(10.37)
India	0.14	(1.78)	0.59	(1.78)	−0.72	(0.05)
Pakistan	0.47	(3.91)	0.93	(3.91)	−0.38	(2.14)
Sri Lanka	7.36	(9.31)	7.84	(9.31)	6.45	(7.45)
Middle East and North Africa						
Algeria[c]	−2.70	(−1.07)	−0.16	(1.39)	−4.49	(−3.41)
Egypt	4.94	(6.73)	7.68	(9.38)	3.02	(4.20)
Jordan	−4.16	(−2.41)	−4.16	(2.02)	−4.98	(−3.69)
Morocco	−1.40	(0.17)	−0.95	(0.57)	−2.24	(−1.14)
Syria[c]	−3.77	(−2.15)	−2.47	(0.90)	−5.26	(−4.16)
Latin America and the Caribbean						
Argentina	−3.92	(−2.69)	−3.48	(−2.30)	−4.74	(−3.97)
Brazil	0.51	(2.20)	0.97	(2.60)	−0.34	(0.85)
Chile	4.75	(6.60)	5.23	(7.03)	3.86	(5.20)
Colombia	−3.94	(−2.29)	−3.51	(−1.90)	−4.76	(−3.57)
Guatemala[c]	−2.96	(−1.13)	−1.65	(0.13)	−4.46	(−3.16)
Mexico	0.21	(1.72)	0.67	(2.13)	−0.64	(0.38)
Peru	0.46	(1.94)	0.92	(2.35)	−0.39	(0.60)

Note: International prices are in U.S. dollars; border prices are in domestic currencies. Border prices are calculated using the formula *WP(XRT/CPI)*, where *WP* is the current world price in U.S. dollars, *XRT* is the nominal exchange rate in local units per U.S. dollar, and *CPI* is the domestic consumer price index. Figures in parentheses are growth rates for 1970–83, excluding 1973 and 1974.
a. Crop year.
b. 1974–83.
c. 1970–81.
Source: Calculations by World Bank Economic Analysis and Projections Department based on data from the IMF and USDA.

Table B-3. Growth in Yields of Cereal, 1960–84
(average annual percentage change)

Region	Years	Wheat	Maize	Rice	Millet	Sorghum
Developing countries	1960–70	3.54	2.47	2.20	3.19	3.53
	1970–84	3.87	2.91	2.44	0.13	1.43
By income						
Low-income Africa	1960–70	2.05	0.04	0.54	0.17	0.16
	1970–84	2.10	0.96	0.09	−1.56	−0.78
Low-income Asia	1960–70	5.14	4.09	2.61	4.59	4.58
	1970–84	4.68	4.62	2.60	0.51	0.64
Middle-income oil importers	1960–70	1.63	2.16	0.67	0.22	3.27
	1970–84	2.42	1.48	1.45	−0.00	3.15
Middle-income oil exporters	1960–70	1.61	1.55	1.44	−0.57	−0.02
	1970–84	1.63	2.39	3.08	2.91	4.11
By region						
East Africa south of Sahara	1960–70	2.28	0.96	1.10	1.11	0.68
	1970–84	2.73	−0.58	−0.42	−1.00	−0.90
West Africa south of Sahara	1960–70	1.10	1.76	0.15	−0.41	−2.87
	1970–84	1.86	−0.26	1.55	0.03	2.31
East Asia and Pacific	1960–70	6.40	4.30	3.30	7.18	8.82
	1970–84	6.38	4.73	2.85	3.58	4.04
South Asia	1960–70	3.59	1.09	0.89	2.05	0.16
	1970–84	2.86	1.03	2.15	1.40	3.20
Middle East and North Africa	1960–70	1.91	5.00	3.29	1.24	−1.13
	1970–84	0.87	1.87	0.96	5.51	−0.48
Latin America and the Caribbean	1960–70	0.47	1.74	−1.33	−2.46	2.09
	1970–84	2.42	2.19	1.64	−0.12	2.58
Industrial market economies	1960–70	2.22	3.67	1.63	−3.77	2.71
	1970–84	1.56	1.88	0.42	0.16	0.29
East-European nonmarket economies	1960–70	4.07	3.94	5.34	2.35	—
	1970–84	0.73	2.81	0.59	−2.37	−1.48

a. U.S.S.R. and Eastern Europe.
Source: World Bank calculations based on USDA data.

Terms of Trade

Table B-4. Terms of Trade for Developing Countries

Country	Exports (average annual percentage change) 1960–70	Exports 1970–82	Imports (average annual percentage change) 1960–70	Imports 1970–82	Terms of trade (1980 = 100) 1970	1979	1983	Purchasing power of exports (1980 = 100) 1970	1979	1983	Merchandise trade, 1982 (millions of dollars) Exports	Imports
Low-income Africa												
Burkina Faso	14.5	9.1	8.1	6.7	134	115	113	70	102	73	80	267
Ghana	0.1	−4.7	−1.5	−4.8	110	137	63	162	104	43	929	703
Kenya	7.5	−3.3	6.5	−2.7	99	108	89	125	113	66	1,125	1,650
Mali	2.9	6.6	−0.4	6.6	120	109	118	58	86	94	93	318
Tanzania	3.8	−5.8	6.0	−1.5	108	106	91	214	129	79	480	1,046
Zaire	−1.7	−5.6	5.4	−12.4	198	114	92	191	100	37	1,713	963
Low-income Asia												
Bangladesh	8.1	−0.8	7.0	5.5	140	99	107	256	105	115	768	2,334
India	4.7	4.7	−0.9	2.6	177	119	98	122	130	108	8,559	16,131
Sri Lanka	4.6	0.1	−0.2	1.8	132	128	98	159	129	123	1,033	1,813
Middle-income oil importers												
Brazil	5.3	8.8	5.0	1.4	169	114	92	73	106	115	20,168	21,069
Chile	0.7	9.5	4.8	1.5	284	115	90	132	115	89	3,836	3,536
Colombia	2.6	2.2	2.4	7.3	82	91	90	60	94	87	2,992	5,359
Guatemala	9.3	5.4	7.2	3.3	126	92	83	82	105	84	1,245	1,340
Jordan	10.8	17.7	3.6	13.5	112	103	101	26	90	112	563	4,897
Korea, Rep. of	34.7	20.2	19.7	9.8	142	128	100	22	117	152	22,251	25,466
Morocco	2.7	−0.3	3.3	4.7	97	115	99	84	105	100	2,130	4,351
Philippines	2.3	7.9	7.2	2.1	207	112	117	102	108	92	5,010	8,229
Senegal	1.4	−1.8	2.3	1.3	101	111	88	134	146	124	482	1,108
Zambia	2.3	−0.5	9.7	−6.8	263	119	82	299	74	84	880	885
Middle-income oil exporters												
Algeria	3.7	−0.3	−1.2	10.8	18	65	102	20	70	93	12,533	10,937
Egypt	3.9	−0.3	−0.9	9.6	98	97	105	102	74	123	3,120	9,077
Indonesia	3.5	4.4	1.9	12.3	26	74	103	18	84	109	20,004	15,647
Mexico	3.4	8.6	6.4	8.7	56	78	105	29	66	153	21,163	15,372
Nigeria	6.6	−1.6	1.5	17.2	19	68	94	15	74	48	14,901	13,902
Peru	2.1	4.8	3.6	1.6	155	100	109	112	114	85	3,196	4,006
Syria	3.5	−4.0	4.1	11.3	23	74	105	38	94	104	1,524	3,567
High-income oil exporters												
Libya	66.0	2.3	15.6	12.9	17	67	98	36	84	57	12,892	8,177

Sources: World Bank, *World Development Report 1984* and UNCTAD (1984).

Table B-5. Terms of Trade for Sub-Saharan Africa

Country	Exports (average annual percentage change) 1960–70	1970–82	Imports (average annual percentage change) 1960–70	1970–82	Terms of trade (1980 = 100) 1970	1979	1983	Purchasing power of exports (1980 = 100) 1970	1979	1983	Merchandise trade, 1982 (millions of dollars) Exports	Imports
Low-income semi-arid												
Burkina Faso	14.5	9.1	8.1	6.7	134	115	113	70	102	73	80	267
Chad	6.0	−8.6	5.1	−3.6	81	101	99	151	150	117	101	132
Mali	2.9	6.6	−0.4	6.6	120	109	118	58	86	94	93	318
Niger	5.9	20.8	12.1	11.0	170	113	112	20	96	67	307	480
Somalia	2.5	9.1	2.7	3.8	157	118	118	84	114	180	143	468
Low-income other												
Benin	5.2	−4.4	7.5	5.2	177	116	75	193	88	57	34	889
Burundi	—	—	—	—	—	—	—	—	—	—	88	214
Central African Rep.	9.6	2.6	4.5	−0.2	106	100	97	86	77	101	106	91
Ethiopia	3.7	1.3	6.2	0.2	156	139	86	132	133	101	400	686
Ghana	0.1	−4.7	−1.5	−4.8	110	137	63	162	104	43	929	703
Guinea	—	—	—	—	—	—	—	—	—	—	411	296
Kenya	7.5	−3.3	6.5	−2.7	99	108	89	125	113	66	1,125	1,650
Madagascar	5.4	−3.6	4.1	−3.4	113	104	93	172	134	77	433	522
Malawi	11.7	5.1	7.6	1.2	138	112	126	74	97	89	232	291
Mozambique	6.0	−13.3	7.9	−14.5	112	104	96	197	94	39	303	792
Rwanda	16.0	2.4	8.2	11.5	79	89	66	114	177	117	82	206
Sierra Leone	2.5	−6.6	1.9	−2.6	146	122	94	202	131	64	169	199
Tanzania	3.8	−5.8	6.0	−1.5	108	106	91	214	129	79	480	1,046
Togo	10.5	0.3	8.6	8.6	73	109	107	60	77	63	213	526
Uganda	6.9	−9.2	6.2	−7.9	92	103	79	276	141	101	371	339
Zaire	−1.7	−5.6	5.4	−12.4	198	114	92	191	100	37	1,713	963
Middle-income oil importers												
Ivory Coast	8.9	2.6	10.0	4.6	110	120	102	65	106	71	2,441	2,094
Liberia	18.5	0.5	2.9	−2.4	189	122	104	161	121	79	1,200	2,463
Mauritania	53.8	−0.1	4.6	3.0	178	103	102	165	92	179	256	445
Senegal	1.4	−1.8	2.3	1.3	101	111	88	134	146	124	482	1,108
Sudan	2.1	−5.1	0.5	3.5	98	99	88	198	114	130	583	1,914
Zambia	2.3	−0.5	9.7	−6.8	263	119	82	299	74	84	880	885
Zimbabwe	—	—	—	—	—	81	105	—	—	—	1,057	1,635
Middle-income oil exporters												
Angola	9.7	−15.8	11.5	0.0	25	75	99	117	62	112	1,730	1,001
Cameroon	7.1	4.0	9.2	5.2	104	120	76	63	97	74	1,721	1,846
Congo, Peoples Rep.	6.4	1.4	−1.0	9.1	18	75	104	12	67	104	923	970
Nigeria	6.6	−1.6	1.5	17.2	19	68	94	15	74	48	14,901	13,902

— Not available.
Sources: World Bank, *World Development Report 1984* and UNCTAD (1984).

Annex C

Econometric Analysis of the Determinants of Food Consumption

Table C-1. Indexes of per Capita Income, Energy Content of the Daily Diet, and Relative Price of Food, 1975
(United States = 100)

Countries classified by per capita income	29 developed and developing countries[a]			17 developing countries[a]		
	Mean income	Mean energy content of diet	Mean relative price of food	Mean income	Mean energy content of diet	Mean relative price of food
Lowest third	12	63	172	8	60	209
Middle third	39	82	137	20	70	125
Highest third	74	101	105	31	81	151
Correlation						
Price/income		$r = -0.56$			$r = -0.40$	
Price/energy		$r = -0.65$			$r = -0.52$	

a. The developed countries included in the analysis are: Austria; Belgium-Luxembourg; Denmark; France; Germany, Fed. Rep.; Ireland; Italy; Japan; Netherlands; Spain; United Kingdom; and the United States. The developing countries included in the analysis are: Brazil, Colombia, India, Iran, Jamaica, Kenya, Korea, Malawi, Malaysia, Mexico, Pakistan, Philippines, Sri Lanka, Syria, Thailand, Uruguay, and Zambia
Source: World Bank data.

Table C-2. Relationship between Energy Content of per Capita Daily Diet and per Capita Income, per Capita Daily Energy Requirements, and the Relative Price of Food across Countries, 1975

	Income elasticity (b_1)	Price elasticity (b_2)	Requirements elasticity (b_3)	R^2
29 developed and developing countries				
Equation 1	0.18 (9.1)	−0.14 (−2.5)		0.88
Equation 2	0.15 (5.9)	−0.09 (−1.6)	0.71 (1.9)	0.89
17 developing countries				
Equation 1	0.16 (6.0)	−0.11 (−2.1)		0.80
Equation 2	0.15 (4.9)	−0.08 (−1.5)	0.43 (0.9)	0.81

Note: Equation 1: $\log C = b_0 + b_1 \log Y + b_2 \log P$
Equation 2: $\log C = b_0 + b_1 \log Y + b_2 \log P + b_3 \log R$

where C = energy content of per capita daily diet
  Y = per capita income valued at purchasing power parity exchange rates
  P = relative price of food index (U.S. = 1.00)
  R = energy requirements of per capita daily diet.

Parentheses indicate t values.
The price of food relative to the prices of all other goods and services was calculated by dividing the purchasing power of a unit of domestic currency spent on food by the purchasing power of a unit of domestic currency spent on all items excluding food.
Sources: Energy content of daily diet, FAO (1980b); per capita income, World Bank data files; relative price of food, Kravis and others (1982); and energy requirement of daily diet, FAO (1977).

Table C-3. Relationship between Growth Rate of the Energy Content of the per Capita Diet, Growth Rates of per Capita Income, and the Self-Sufficiency Ratio of Cereal Supplies, for Fifty-three Developing Countries in Which More Than 40 Percent of All Food Energy Is Derived from Cereals, 1970–80

	(b_1)	(b_2)	(b_3)	(b_4)	R^2
Equation 1	0.18 (6.0)				0.40
Equation 2	−0.82 (3.6)	−0.74 (−3.0)	0.00004 (3.2)		0.55
Equation 3	−0.84 (3.6)	−0.75 (−3.1)	0.00004 (3.2)	0.018 (1.4)	0.57

Note: Equation 1: $Y = b_0 X_1^{b_1}$
Equation 2: $Y = b_0 X_1^{b_1 + b_2 X_2 + b_3 X_3}$
Equation 3: $Y = b_0 X_1^{b_1 + b_2 X_2 + b_3 X_3} X_4^{b_4}$

where Y = growth rate of energy in daily per capita diet, 1970–80 (FAO)
  X_1 = growth rate of per capita income, 1970–80 (World Bank)
  X_2 = ratio of energy consumption to requirements, 1969–71 average (FAO)
  X_3 = per capita gross domestic product valued at purchasing power parity exchange rates, 1969–71 average (World Bank)
  X_4 = growth rate in self-sufficiency ratio of cereal supply, 1970–80 (USDA).

The countries are listed on Table C-5.
Parentheses indicate t values.

Table C-4. Estimating Equations of Energy Content in per Capita National Diet for Fifty-three Developing Countries in Which More Than 40 Percent of All Food Energy Is Derived from Cereals, 1976–80

Region	Income elasticity (b_1)	Self-sufficiency elasticity (b_2)	R^2
All countries (53)	0.14 (8.5)	0.005 (0.2)	0.61
Africa (22)	0.13 (4.3)	0.001 (0.1)	0.50
Asia (11)	0.17 (3.9)	−0.039 (−0.5)	0.75
Latin America and the Caribbean (11)	0.18 (2.7)	0.010 (0.3)	0.51
Middle East and North Africa (9)	0.19 (4.0)	0.110 (1.6)	0.74

Note: The estimating equation is:
$$\log Y = b_0 + b_1 \log X_1 + b_2 \log X_2$$
where Y = the energy in the per capita daily diet
X_1 = per capita income (purchasing power parity)
X_2 = the self-sufficiency ratio in cereals supply.
The countries are listed in Table C-5.
Parentheses indicate *t* values.

Table C-5. Fifty-three Developing Countries in Which More Than 40 Percent of All Food Energy Is Derived from Cereals

Afghanistan	Mali
Algeria	Mauritania
Bangladesh	Mexico
Botswana	Morocco
Burkina Faso	Nepal
Burma	Nicaragua
Chad	Niger
Chile	Nigeria
Egypt	Pakistan
El Salvador	Panama
Ethiopia	Peru
Gambia	Philippines
Guatemala	Senegal
Guyana	Sierra Leone
Honduras	Somalia
India	Sri Lanka
Indonesia	Sudan
Iran	Suriname
Iraq	Swaziland
Jordan	Syria
Kenya	Thailand
Korea, Rep. of	Trinidad and Tobago
Lesotho	Tunisia
Liberia	Turkey
Libya	Zambia
Malawi	Zimbabwe
Malaysia	

References

Ahluwalia, Montek. 1976. "Inequality, Poverty, and Development." *Journal of Development Economics,* vol. 3, pp. 307–42. Also available as World Bank Reprint Series no. 36.

Ahluwalia, Montek, Nicolas B. Carter, and Hollis Chenery. 1979. *Growth and Poverty in Developing Countries.* Washington, D.C.: World Bank.

Alderman, Harold, and Joachim von Braun. 1984. *The Effects of the Egyptian Food Ration and Subsidy System on Income Distribution and Consumption.* Research Report no. 45. Washington, D.C.: IFPRI.

Bale, Malcolm D., and Ronald C. Duncan. 1983. *Prospects for Food Production and Consumption in Developing Countries.* World Bank Staff Working Paper no. 596. Washington, D.C.

Beaton, George H. 1982. "Some Thoughts on the Definition of the World Nutrition Problem." Paper presented at the 8th Session of the UN Administrative Committee of Coordination, Subcommittee on Nutrition, Bangkok, Thailand. Processed.

————. 1983. "Energy in Human Nutrition," W.O. Atwater Memorial Lecture. *Nutrition Today,* vol. 18, no. 5 (September/October).

Berg, Alan. 1981. *Malnourished People: A Policy View.* Poverty and Basic Needs Series. Washington, D.C.: The World Bank.

Binswanger, Hans, and Jaime Quizon. 1984a. "Distributional Consequences of Alternative Food Policies in India." Report no. ARU 20, Agriculture and Rural Development Department, World Bank, Washington, D.C.

————. 1984b. "Income Distribution in India—The Impact of Policies and Growth in the Agricultural Sector." Report no. ARU 21, Agriculture and Rural Development Department, World Bank, Washington, D.C.

Brown, Lester R. 1984. "Securing Food Supplies." In *State of the World—1984.* New York: W. W. Norton and Company.

Centro Internacional de Agricultura Tropical (CIAT). 1983. *Report 1983.* Cali, Colombia.

Chenery, Hollis B., and Moises Syrquin. 1975. *Patterns of Development, 1950–1970.* New York: Oxford University Press.

Coyle, W. 1983. *Japan's Feed Livestock Economy.* Washington, D.C.: USDA.

de Janvry, A., and K. Subbarao. 1984. *Agricultural Price Policy and Income Distribution.* Working Paper no. 274. Berkeley, Calif. Giannini Foundation of Agricultural Economics.

Economist Intelligence Unit. 1983. *World Commodity Outlook 1984: Food, Feedstuffs and Beverages.* London.

Food and Agriculture Organization (FAO). 1977. *Fourth World Food Survey.* Rome.

————. 1980a. *Agriculture: Towards 2000.* Rome.

---. 1980b. *Food Balance Sheets and Per Capita Food Supplies*. Rome.

---. 1982. *Statistics on Prices Received by Farmers*. Rome.

---. 1983a. *Changing Patterns and Trends in Feed Utilization*. Economic and Social Development Paper no. 37. Rome.

---. 1983b. *Food Outlook Supplement*. Rome.

---. 1985. *Fifth World Food Survey*. Rome.

---. *Production Yearbook*. Rome, various years.

---. *Trade Yearbook*. Rome, various issues.

Goreux, Louis. 1980. *Compensatory Financing Facility*. IMF Pamphlet no. 34. Washington, D.C.: IMF.

Hazell, Peter. 1984. "Sources of Increased Variability in World Cereal Production Since the 1960s." IFPRI, Washington, D.C. Processed.

Huddleston, Barbara, D. Gale Johnson, Shlomo Reutlinger, and Alberto Valdes. 1984. *International Finance for Food Security*. Baltimore, Md.: Johns Hopkins University Press.

Huddleston, Barbara, and Panos Konandreas. 1981. "Insurance Approach to Food Security: Simulation of Benefits for 1970/71–76/77 and for 1978–82." In Alberto Valdes, ed., *Food Security for Developing Countries*. Boulder, Col.: Westview Press.

International Crops Research Institute for the Semi-Arid Tropics (ICRISAT). 1982. *Annual Report, 1981*. Andra Pradesh, India.

International Wheat Council. 1983. *Long Term Grain Outlook*. London.

Johnson, D. Gale. 1976. "Increased Stability of Grain Supplies in Developing Countries: Optimal Carryover and Insurance." *World Development*, vol. 4, pp. 977–87.

Konandreas, Panos, Barbara Huddleston, and V. Ramankuro. 1978. *Food Security: An Insurance Approach*. Research Report no. 4. Washington, D.C.: IFPRI.

Kravis, Irving B., Alan Heston, and Robert Summers. 1982. *World Product and Income: International Comparisons of Real GDP*. Baltimore, Md.: Johns Hopkins University Press.

Kuznets, Simon. 1975. "Demographic Aspects of Size Distribution of Income: An Exploratory Essay." *Economic Development and Cultural Change*. vol. 25, (October).

Mellor, John W. 1978. "The Food Price Policy and Income Distribution in Low Income Countries." *Economic Development and Cultural Change*, vol. 27, no. 1 (October).

Monke, Eric. 1983. "International Grain Trade, 1950–80." AGREP Division Working Paper, no. 64. Agriculture and Rural Development Department, World Bank, Washington, D.C.

India, National Council of Applied Economic Research. 1975. *Changes in Rural Income Survey*. New Delhi.

Newberry, David, and Joseph Stiglitz. 1981. *The Theory of Commodity Price Stabilization: A Study in the Economics of Risk*. Oxford: Clarendon Press.

Offutt, S. 1982. *The Impact of Export Instability on the U.S. Corn and Livestock Markets: An Econometric Analysis*. Ithaca, New York: Department of Agricultural Economics, Cornell University.

Paulino, Leonardo. 1984. *Food in the Third World: Past Trends and Projections to 2000*. Washington, D.C.: IFPRI.

Pinstrup-Andersen, Per. 1983. *Export Crop Production and Malnutrition*. Occasional Paper Series, vol. 11, no. 10 (February). Institute of Nutrition. University of North Carolina.

Reutlinger, Shlomo. 1977. *Food Insecurity: Magnitude and Remedies*. World Bank Staff Working Paper no. 267. Washington, D.C.

---. 1983a. "Changes in the Energy Content of National Diets and in the Energy Deficient Diets of the Poor: 1970–1980." World Bank, Washington, D.C. Processed.

---. 1983b. "Nutritional Impact of Agricultural Projects: Conceptual Framework. "In *Nutritional Impact of Agricultural Projects*. Papers and proceedings of a workshop held by the United Nations Inter-Agency Subcommittee on Nutrition. Rome: IFAD.

Reutlinger, Shlomo, and Marcelo Selowsky. 1976. *Malnutrition and Poverty: Magnitude and Policy Options*. World Bank Staff Occasional Paper no. 23. Baltimore, Md.: Johns Hopkins University Press.

Richardson, J., and D. Ray. 1979. "Demand for Feedgrains and Concentrates by Livestock Category." *Western Journal of Agricultural Economics*, vol. 3, no. 1 (June).

Sanderson, Fred H. 1984. *Global Demand for Food and Fiber through 2000*. Washington, D.C.: Resources for the Future.

Schuh, G. Edward. 1984. "Third Country Marketing Distortions in a Changed International Economy: The Case of Brazil and Mexico." Paper prepared for the 75th American Colloquium of the Harvard Business School, April 8–11, 1984, Cambridge, Mass. Processed.

Schultz, Theodore W. 1979. *The Economics of Being*

Poor. Nobel Lecture. Stockholm, Sweden: Carolinske Institute.

Scobie, Grant M. 1984. *Food Subsidies in Egypt: Their Impact on Foreign Exchange and Trade.* Research Report no. 40. Washington, D.C.: IFPRI.

Sen, Amartya K. 1981. *Poverty and Famines: An Essay on Entitlement and Deprivation.* Oxford: Clarendon Press.

Singer, Hans, and S.J. Maxwell. 1983. "Development through Food Aid: Twenty Years' Experience." Report of the World Food Programme, Government of the Netherlands Seminar on Food Aid, The Hague.

Sri Lanka, Ministry of Plan Information. 1982. *The Evaluation Report on the Food Stamp Scheme.* No. 7, Colombo.

Timmer, C. Peter, Walter Falcon, and Scott Pearson. 1983. *Food Policy Analysis.* Baltimore, Md.: Johns Hopkins University Press.

United Nations Conference on Trade and Development (UNCTAD). 1984. *Handbook of International Trade and Development Statistics.* Geneva.

United States Department of Agriculture (USDA). 1984a. *World Agricultural Supply and Demand Estimates.* Washington, D.C.

———. 1984b. *World Food Situation and Prospects to 2000: Factors Affecting Supply.* Washington, D.C.: USDA Economic Research Service.

Vu, My T. 1984. *World Population Projections 1984.* Washington, D.C.: World Bank.

Wheeler, Richard, and others. 1981. *The World Livestock Product, Feedstuff, and Food Grain System.* Marrilton, Ark.: Winrock International.

Williamson Gray, Cheryl. 1982. *Food Consumption Parameters for Brazil and Their Application to Food Policy.* Research Report no. 32. Washington, D.C.: IFPRI.

World Bank. 1983. *Commodity Trade and Price Trends.* Washington, D.C.

———. 1984. "1984 Survey of Country Economists." Economic Analysis and Projections Department. World Bank, Washington, D.C. Processed.

———. 1985. *World Development Report 1985* and various other issues. New York: Oxford University Press.

World Health Organization. 1973. *Energy and Protein Requirements.* Report of a Joint FAO/WHO *ad hoc* expert committee. WHO Technical Report Series no. 522. Geneva.

The most recent World Bank publications are described in the annual spring and fall lists. The latest edition is available free of charge from Publications Sales Unit, Department B, The World Bank, Washington, D.C. 20433, U.S.A.